DUDE,
YOU'RE A
DAD!

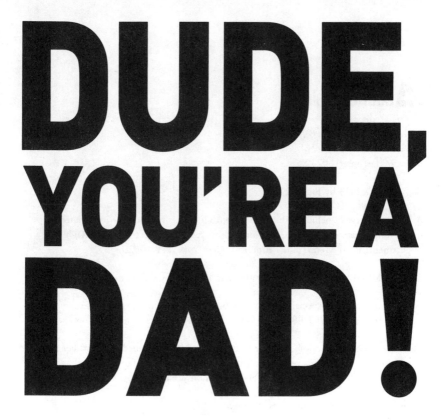

DUDE, YOU'RE A DAD!

How to Get (All of You) Through Your Baby's First Year

JOHN PFEIFFER

Author of the bestselling
Dude, You're Gonna Be a Dad!

Adams Media
New York London Toronto Sydney New Delhi

Adams Media
An Imprint of Simon & Schuster, Inc.
57 Littlefield Street
Avon, Massachusetts 02322

For information about special discounts for bulk purchases, please contact Simon & Schuster Special Sales at 1-866-506-1949 or business@simonandschuster.com.

The Simon & Schuster Speakers Bureau can bring authors to your live event. For more information or to book an event contact the Simon & Schuster Speakers Bureau at 1-866-248-3049 or visit our website at www.simonspeakers.com.

Manufactured in the United States of America

10 9 8

Library of Congress Cataloging-in-Publication Data has been applied for.

ISBN 978-1-4405-4112-4

ISBN 978-1-4405-4793-5 (ebook)

Dedication

"It is not the critic who counts: not the man who points out how the strong man stumbles or where the doer of deeds could have done better. The credit belongs to the man who is actually in the arena, whose face is marred by dust and sweat and blood, who strives valiantly, who errs and comes up short again and again, because there is no effort without error or shortcoming, but who knows the great enthusiasms, the great devotions, who spends himself for a worthy cause; who, at the best, knows, in the end, the triumph of high achievement, and who, at the worst, if he fails, at least he fails while daring greatly, so that his place shall never be with those cold and timid souls who knew neither victory nor defeat." —THEODORE ROOSEVELT

To those who just experienced the miracle of childbirth—
I dedicate this book to you. Welcome to the parenting "arena."

Acknowledgments

So, who needs thanking? Thanks to my family, you knew I could write a book before I did. To Alana and my kids, Kaitlyn, Lindsay, and Zoey, let's go on vacation and never come back! To Brendan, for your input and course correction skills. Thanks to my editor Katie, for your expert editing touch. To Adams Media, I appreciate the chance, and would love to do it again.

Contents

Introduction

Now that you are home from the hospital, things just got *real*. Remember all of the changes and challenges people have told you are coming? Well, they have arrived. So whether you find yourself totally accepting all of the major changes coming to your world, have totally put off thinking about these changes, or are totally terrified of what's coming, *Dude, You're a Dad!* is going to try to get things moving forward as smoothly as possible. From the jump it will be important to be mindful of something: you are but one member of the team. The three of you are now tied together by the unseen (love, family) and all of you rise and fall together with the tide. If you experience success, you all share in it. The opposite is true as well. So whether the purchase of this book was a simple review of parenting basics or a cry for help, there is only one thing left to do: get down to business.

In a perfect world, you could handle everything that life throws at you with style and aplomb. You could sit behind your stately desk in your office and pass judgment on everything from that night's dinner menu to Saturday's proposed schedule with nothing but a "thumbs up" or "thumbs down." In reality though, once you introduce children into your lives, chaos ensues. Maybe your BMP (baby-making partner, of course!) is out of town and junior wakes up sick. Hmmm. Looks like you better know how understanding your boss *really* is. But no matter the situation, it is time to redefine what control is and embrace the chaos that comes with being interdependent on other family members in your life.

What does this have to do with being a dad? The journey of fatherhood began at the fertilization of your BMP's egg—learn more in *Dude, You're Gonna Be a Dad!* Haven't read it? You're missing out!—and has shifted into a whole new gear now that the baby is here. The type of father and partner that you decide to be will have a huge impact on the health and well-being of everyone in your family. And lots of the information and advice contained within these pages is going to have one of two common themes: 1) giving of yourself (which will be easier for some and harder for others) and 2) taking care of yourself. (If you do not take care of yourself, then the daily responsibilities you tackle each and every day will wear on you, and you will lose perspective.) But the simplest and best advice I can give you is to have a plan and stay informed.

As for the plan, whether you use a calendar that you drew with a crayon or a virtual calendar accessible from your phone, computer, and tablet, make sure that you have something to keep you straight and organized. Find something that works for you, that renews your spirit and drive every day, and keep to it. Some dads I know keep a detailed five-year plan. Others read daily inspirations to get their day started. And some are simply hanging on for dear life. As for the staying informed, you simply need to carve a few minutes of time out of your day to explore all of the information out there. Well, not *all* of it, as there is virtually a limitless number of books, websites, magazines, blogs, etc. to choose from (see the resource list at the back of the book for some info on where to start). Really what you need to do is consume, digest, and process. Take the information available, see if you think it is something you believe, and decide if you are going to incorporate it into your family life. I hope to help you achieve a strong first step toward these goals with this book. Yes, you will be giving lots of your time, emotional strength, and patience to your parental duties. But, whatever the method, you need to find a way to renew your strength and fervor to tackle the challenges headed your way. Yoga? Running? Meditation? Book club? I don't know what drives you, but find a positive outlet for yourself that renews your strength and energy. It will save you a lot of headaches, and potentially thousands in therapy. But with everything that will be happening in your world, you will need to find a system that works.

How are you to put all of this advice into practice? Throughout *Dude, You're a Dad!*, you'll find all the pertinent information you need to execute your parenting plan. In addition, you'll find Crib Notes chapter summaries in case you need to go back in for a refresher course, quotes from famous parents to put things into perspective, and "It's a Fact, Baby!" sidebars that will help you learn important new baby trivia as you work your way through your baby's first year. So put a fresh diaper on your child and brew a pot of coffee. It's time to start learning.

PART I

Months 1–3

By now the realization may have occurred to you that modern parenting involves a lot of planning, organization, and to-do lists. While your wife was pregnant you had to plan your trip to the hospital, figure out what needed to go in the "hospital bag," manage the grandparents and various family members, and start to introduce your pet to the fact that he is going to be lower in the family rank from now on. All that, and your child hadn't even been born yet! Well, as an experienced parent, I am here to tell you something important: make sure to take some time to yourselves in these precious first months and just enjoy each other as a family. Set aside the time to take a walk together or just be together. It will be the first step in bonding together as a family. Soon your lives will be full of some of the practical issues we will be discussing like how you safely hold your child, visiting the doctor's office with your child (again and again!), as well as what to be on the lookout for if an outside caregiver is needed for your child. But as a starting point to building a deeper bond with your family, let's take some time to get to know more about your baby, Mommy, and even yourself—as a dad.

CHAPTER 1

(All Together Now) Getting to Know You . . .

You have a new family member! This in and of itself is very exciting. Now, I'm sure that there are some of you out there—and I don't want to name names—who are sitting comfortably on the couch and waiting for all of the baby information and expertise to be inserted into your brain the way Keanu Reeves's character learned jujitsu in *The Matrix*. That would certainly be nice, but as of right now you are still powering the mainframe and will not receive such knowledge. Life is messy, and the best way to get something out of it is to get in there and experience it in all of its glory. The same goes for your relationship with your new child. Learn as much as you can, take the red pill, and then simply jump in with both feet.

Meet Your Baby

First we need to take a step back and admire the brilliant engineering miracle that is the human body. The amazing human body, in its adult form, consists of about 206 bones, is directed by a brain that generates the same amount of power as a 10-watt light bulb, and sends out thought impulses that travel as fast as 170 miles per hour. Your brain regulates your body temperature, tells you when you need more fuel, and stores tons of readily available information for you to access. Man and our incredible brains have built the pyramids of Egypt, walked on the moon, and brought us those cute "cat plays the piano while wearing sunglasses" web videos. And all of this greatness comes from a one-time single cell organism that, at various points in its existence, could not perform basic functions like clothing or feeding itself.

Make no mistake about why these babies are here—

they are here to replace us.

—Jerry Seinfeld

Your baby is at that helpless time in its life, and truly needs your help. Much like Microsoft does with its software, the human body usually sends the baby out into the marketplace not quite fully formed, but functional. When babies are born, they actually have 300 bones, which need time to fuse and mature into the adult skeleton with its aforementioned 206 skeletal bones. In addition, you may begin to wonder why a baby's brain sends out the signal to cry—all the time—but the truth of the matter is that your baby is only screaming and hollering; he cannot produce tears until he is at least three weeks old (don't you feel better?). Truth be told, you are responsible for the creation of this person (religious considerations notwithstanding) and are going to take care of him until he can fend for himself, somewhere between eighteen and thirty years from now. Your list of responsibilities includes providing food, clothing, shelter, and hopefully some sort of direction and purpose to your newborn before you send him off into the cruel world by himself.

It's a Fact, Baby!

True or False: Your child can recognize its parents' faces.

False. It takes a few weeks for your baby to recognize your and mom's faces. But a child recognizes the voice and smell of its mother from birth.

In the meantime, your child has a lot to learn. While all of the body parts and muscles are there from the beginning, it takes some time and practice for a baby to get used to operating a machine as complicated as the human body. Even the simple act of walking takes the coordination of almost 200 different muscles. And once your child is able to master the complex series of thought and coordination of muscles required to do this, he will just be getting started. But your baby is also a multitasker: while learning to coordinate and move all of these different body parts, he is also getting started on learning the approximately 1 million words that Webster estimates make up the English language, starting with "Mama" and "Dada" and quickly followed by the word "No." The point here is there is more growth and develop-ment going on when your child is an infant and toddler than in any other time in his life. This is quite an exciting time, full of victories and cute failures, and you will have a front row seat. So while your nose may be offended from time to time, don't forget to keep in mind what an amazing thing the growth and development of your child really is.

How to Handle Your Baby (With Care)

Now, just in case you are feeling nervous about holding your child, or if you just need a quick refresher on what to do, here are a few tips on how to handle your child correctly when Mom leaves you in charge:

- **Heads Up:** Your baby's head is too big for his body, and the neck muscles are not strong enough to support his massive melon. So when you hold Junior, make sure you give his head plenty of support.
- **You Big Softie:** Your child does have a soft spot or two on his scalp; these spots are called fontanelles. Just so you know, it's okay to touch, wash, or stroke these spots. There is a spot in the back of the head that hardens generally by the time an infant reaches two months of age. The one most people generally think of, on the top of the head, will not close or harden until your baby reaches about eighteen months of age.
- **Get a Grip:** When putting your child in or out of the bath, it's important to have a good grip. Keeping one hand behind the shoulders and supporting the head, and the other underneath, is generally accepted as the most secure way to move a wet, wiggly baby.

So there you go. You can now safely handle your little one without fear of damaging or (gasp!) dropping him. The next step in the revolution will be to teach parents to keep track of their kids at the mall without the use of leashes.

From BMP to BRP—Here's Mommy

Many of you may be familiar with the term "BMP," or "baby-making partner." You know, the mother of your child. Let's hope you not only know her, but care deeply for her. This is not just the romantic in me talking; a stable relationship between parents has been proven to help the successful emotional development of children. The research here from the National Society for Children and Family Contact (nscfc.com) is pretty indisputable. Consider this:

- 70 percent of young offenders come from lone parent families
- Children of lone parents are twice as likely to have mental health problems
- Children of lone parents are twice as likely to smoke, drink, or take drugs
- Children of lone parents are *five* times more likely to suffer physical and emotional abuse

The more you look, the more you will find facts like this. My only gripe is their use of the term "lone" parent. In the simplest terms, parenting is a tough go, and being the breadwinner, chauffeur, disciplinarian, etc. to children all rolled into one is asking a lot of one person.

So the evidence is there that Mom needs you, and you need her. Mom, also known as your BRP? You remember her? She has a really engaging personality, looks that caught your eye, and a beautiful soul that allows the two of you to connect on many levels. Now the romantic in me is taking over. Anyway . . .

That was your BMP. But the two of you have been through the life-changing experience of bringing a child into the world together. You were definitely part of it, but her body did most of the work. Going through a major life event like that often changes people, and your BMP has changed. All of those wonderful qualities that you love about her are still in the mix, but starting now, she will be growing and changing as she takes on the role of being a mother. She is now your "BRP," or "baby-raising partner." Life experience and the responsibility of having a child will apply a smooth finish to her as she eases into becoming both a woman *and* a mom. "What is going to be the difference?" you may be asking yourself. You and she talked about how you would still do all of your favorite things together. Eat at your favorite restaurants, go to the movies, go see your favorite local bands play. But, although I don't have an advanced medical degree, I believe there is a term for this type of thinking, where you promise yourself that a major life change is not going to change you.

It's called denial.

I am not referring to the rather large river in Africa. I am talking about the fact that you are not being realistic with yourself. Having children changes a woman; it will change you, and it will change your relationship. Your children will expose and introduce you to aspects of yourself that you never knew existed. You may not even realize this until you are getting up in the face of a parent whose toddler pushed your child down on the playground; while you are barely resisting the urge to squirt breastmilk at the parent of the offender, you may wonder, "Where did this come from? I'm not usually like this." Well, it came from the change you undergo when you become a parent. Let's look at some of the changes new parents often experience. For the change applying to Dad, I speak from firsthand experience. For the female side of the ledger, I can cobble together a few important issues I have noticed from relevant sources including my own experience with my wife, discussions with others, and, of course, my keen observational powers:

- **Shifting Priorities:** Your mama grizzly may or may not run for office, but she will feel protective toward her cubs. In fact, they will probably become her top priority, where other things (including you) get pushed down the list. "What is best for your child" will be the lens through which decisions are made, while questions like "Does Daddy need a new iPhone?" may be further down the list.
- **Quality of Life:** What this means to you and your family will be different. Maybe a smaller house and a smaller budget is an easy tradeoff to working closer to home, having a shorter commute, and spending more time with your child. I'm going to go out on a limb here: women usually adjust first. Whether it's the physical reinforcement of carrying the baby or something else, women seem to be ready to shift resources to the child. Sometimes, Dads, we tend to be a little more resistive (just think of the "man cave" trend).
- **Relationships:** As you now have a new, very time-intensive family member, you—and your BRP—will have less time to have other relationships. Your old college friend or former coworker may call you

up and say, "Where you been?" You may also look to your parents and ask, "How did you do it?" Both you and your BRP will be experiencing changes in almost every single relationship you currently have. Some will grow, some may wither, and new ones will form. There may be casualties, but that is why your relationship with Mom is so important—you need to be there for one another no matter what.

- **Emotions in Motion:** It does seem from my experience, and from my time spent perusing motherhood websites, that there is a change that happens here emotionally. Moms often say that their emotions become more intense. There may be a more frequent onslaught of tears. You may see tears during movies, Hallmark-channel movies, heck even during commercials.

- **Redefining "Control":** New parents often report that their definition of control changes—as in, they really don't have much control over their baby at all. If the baby wants to eat, sleep, or throw a fit, it doesn't matter where you are or what you *had* planned. Embracing this fluid, always-changing way of going about your life takes some getting used to, but if you learn to roll with the chaos, and realize that no plans are ever truly set in stone, you will save yourself some frustration. Dinners, movies, and trips to the mall are all subject to being rescheduled. The best and only way to ensure completion is to have a trusted babysitter take over for a little while. If you invite your mother-in-law over just so you can catch up on yard work, you're experiencing fatherhood in its full bloom. Depending on how much both of you like routine in your lives, or how strictly you set and follow a plan, this may be a significant change in both of your lives.

- **Fashion Will Go Out the Window**: You are pouring lots of time, energy, and yes, money into the care of your child. Whether or not the two of you are dressed in "the latest" will not be as important. This also applies to your general vanity in all areas. Most of the free time you get will usually be spent catching up with housework, yard work, etc.—all of the little things that may slide when you introduce such a large (but wonderful) change into your lives. That four-mile jog may get traded in for forty-five minutes of sleep instead.

- **In Hindsight**: Becoming a parent will drastically change the way you look at your own childhood—and at your parents. Once you "cross over" to the parent side of the ledger, having to balance the interests and greater goods for multiple family members, you may be more inclined to cut your own parents some slack. Navigation of the quagmire that is raising a child is no easy task. How can you teach the "secret of life" to your child when you haven't figured it out for yourself? As new parents, you are on uncharted ground. There is no real way to train; the learning of a parent is almost exclusively of the "on the job" variety. It may be a real change for you to tackle something this new, where there are many tips and tricks but very few rules, but don't get overwhelmed and keep at it! You will find a system that works for you and your family.

So, as you can see, there is quite a lot going on here in early parenthood, just like there is so much going on with your child. It can get messy with multiple family members changing so rapidly, so try to keep things in perspective. A former manager of mine used to say that we were not encountering "problems"; we were simply finding "opportunities." You may be finding many "opportunities" that will stretch your patience and your ability to keep a level head, but you'll have to get used to change in your life and adjust accordingly, because change is the only thing that will be a constant in your life going forward. And speaking of change, we will be discussing the many changes that Junior will go through (all throughout, but there's a lot of detailed information contained in Chapter 5) as well as how your partner might be changing (skip ahead to Chapter 6 if you must). Hmm. Is there anyone else? I can't help but feel that we are forgetting somebody . . .

It's a Fact, Baby!

True or False: Newborn babies sleep more than twelve hours a day.

True. Newborn babies actually sleep an average of 16–17 hours a day. It may just not seem like it to you, because they usually get their rest one to two hours at a time.

This Is *You* as a Father

The word "Dad," as far as the experts can tell, actually came from babies themselves, but almost every older language has some form of the word "father." It is actually "Vader" in old German. If only I would have known this when *Star*

Wars was released, I might have pieced it all together and been the coolest kid in grade school. But no matter what language your child uses to address you, you are her dad, and you have an important job to do. Now, I'm sure you've heard that the job is quite a challenge; in fact, cynics out there label parenting as an exercise in failure and say that, as a parent, you can only strive to fail less than the next parent. While I am cynical on many fronts, I respectfully disagree.

By the time a man realizes that maybe his father was right,

he usually has a son who thinks he's wrong.

—Charles Wadsworth, 1814–1882

I have seen the relationship and the connection between parent and child gradually change, but what remains constant is the love between them. Perhaps we can meet on some middle ground with the cynics and all agree on this: parenting is hard—and in some ways, the changes that men experience catch us by surprise. Your body did not go through the same things that your BRP's did, and often times men do not realize the degree to which they will be changing. Hopefully the outcome is more like a strike of lightning spurring you on to the next phase of your life, and less like a car crash. Now, if you're not sure how to define who you are or what to do as a parent right now, here are some of the basics to help you get started:

- **Just Be There:** Children who have a father around when they are growing up have more positive relationships, and those without a father in their lives

adopt all sorts of negative behaviors and tend to suffer from emotional instability. And, in addition to
you, your child needs your BRP. It's true: kids need
both parents. It has been pretty well documented that
this is the best-case scenario for children to grow into
healthy adults (though not the only scenario). The
balance, love, and support that children receive from
two involved parents give them not only the tools and
advice they need, but also a solid example to follow
on how to overcome life's many obstacles. But if you
are reading this book, you are probably already committed, so way to go! I thought it wouldn't hurt to
give you a pat on the back anyway.

- **Security:** You are your child's protector, and your
  children need to feel safe and secure and to know that
  you will provide for them and that you will be there
  to protect them from the monsters under the bed. If a
  problem or threat arises, your children know you will
  take care of it. Nobody is tougher than Daddy!

- **Understand Your Child:** Nobody knows your child
  the way that you do. You may understand her special
  language when she first begins talking, just like you
  will have insight into her heart when she gets older.
  You will know and understand her hopes and nurture
  her dreams, just like you know what type of baby food
  she prefers. As a parent, you can provide both the carrot
  of hope and the stick of discipline to guide your child.

- **Set Boundaries:** You are the one who will teach
  your children about what is acceptable behavior and
  what isn't. Some children always call adults "sir" or
  "ma'am." Others treat you like they are your equal
  and address you as "dude" or "bro." While in some

homes a "C" report-card grade is an instant ground-
ing, in others it's just no big deal. Since your child
cannot even speak yet, you have a little time to decide
which of these things are important to you. But as
parents, you set the tone and limitations for your children and in many ways set the agenda for their lives.

- **Coping Skills:** If you are simply a restaurant, hotel, and
  ATM to your child, then you are missing the boat. You
  need to teach him how to deal with success and failure,
  and put him on the track to adulthood. Sometimes—
  especially when you know that your child will fail at
  something and just have to let him do it anyway—
  these situations fly in the face of your protective parental instincts. But the younger your child is, the easier it
  is to clean up the mess. Little kids have little problems,
  in other words, and it is easier to recover from striking
  out in a Little League game than it is to recover from
  striking out with your high school crush. So let him
  get out there and experience life a little bit, and learn
  to deal with the highs and lows. By the way, you'll need
  to develop these skills for yourself as well. Life is uncer-
  tain and if you or your spouse are unexpectedly laid off
  from work, or face a scary medical situation, you need
  to be able to cope, stay mentally strong, and overcome
  these obstacles as a family.

So you see, it's going to be really easy, right? Everyone
in your family will be constantly experiencing both positive and negative changes in their lives. Change is always
tough. Each family member will be dealing with his or her
own trials, and all the while you will have to balance the
wants and needs of each person, along with the financial

considerations every family faces. At least one parent (hopefully) will also be dealing with the issues that can arise from working a job, and *somebody* still needs to get to the grocery store . . . I think you get the point. As a parent you will constantly be juggling, juggling, juggling, and distributing limited resources of time, talent, and treasure among multiple important family members. It is a challenging task that can—and likely will—take some time to master. But for all of that hard work, there is a lifetime of rewards. Just talk to your parents and/or grandparents about their lives. The consistent refrain among them is not that they regret not working more or advancing further in their career. What they cherish are the good times with their family, and they often regret that there are not more of those good times to look back on. Do you remember the look on the grandparents' faces when they first held your little baby? I do. What I saw was a look of pride and joy.

The life of a family is a world where you must always look at the entire family and balance and prioritize resources of time, talent, and treasure. Does this juggling act that I just described sound fun and challenging? I hope so, because this is *you*, learning to be a dad and striving for those special life rewards that come with doing your job well.

It's a Fact, Baby!

True or False: There is now a diaper bag for men.

False. There is a diaper bag that is being *marketed* to men, but there is truly no men's diaper bag by the mere function of the bag itself. You can create a "murse" (man purse), but that does not mean that the Committee of Grown Men sanctions the use of this item.

Chapter 1

Crib Notes

- Babies, along with humans in general, are an engineering marvel.
- The act of walking engages over 200 muscles, so it will take your child a while to master it. Be patient!
- If you are at all nervous about handling your child, make sure you look up the most secure way to hold and support him—especially when putting him in and taking him out of the bath.
- The arrival of your child will bring about several changes in your life, and change the relationship with your partner/BMP.
- Parenting is a really tough job. Although there will be times you feel like it's overwhelming, just the fact that you are there giving it your all will have a positive impact on your child in the long run.
- Spend a few minutes thinking about what kind of father you want to be. Begin to define what is a priority to you.

CHAPTER 2

Home Sweet Home

As the old saying goes, home is where the heart is, and there is a strong statistical possibility that your child and her mom are here as well. Remember back in those bachelor days when you had a date come over? You prepared to impress by cleaning up all of the pizza boxes and hiding all of the dirty laundry. You swept up and even sprayed some Lysol to kill the smell of sweaty socks. Well, now that you are a family man, it is time to raise your game and prepare your home a little more thoroughly for your child, so let's review some of the ways that you can ensure your home is ready and safe for your baby.

Preparing Your Home for Tiny New Residents

If you are like some dads I know, finishing the baby's new nursery was one of your "to-dos" before your child was born. But if your child's arrival was early or it just, um, "snuck up on you" (wasn't her growing tummy a hint?), then you still have some work to do. As if your "honey do" list wasn't already long enough! When the final coat of paint in the nursery is dry, here are some other areas to turn your attention toward:

It's a Fact, Baby!

Who is stronger, pound for pound—your baby or an ox?

Your baby is stronger! Especially her little legs. Technically, when they measure "pound for pound," which must be some sort of crazy math trick, like the way the interest on your credit card is charged, babies are stronger. That is why they need to be in car seats and the cabinets must be babyproofed. These little guys are stronger than you think.

Babyproofing

I hope you've at least got the basics down on this one. Yes, I know your baby cannot yet move. But at some point, he will gain the ability to transport himself around the house, a skill that comes coupled with the innate ability to find trouble. If you've ever owned a puppy, it might give you a glimpse. To get an idea of what you're in for, get down on all fours and crawl around your house to see what your child will see. It might just give you a new perspective on your life, or maybe it will just gross you out how dirty your carpet is. But it will definitely help you approximate what your baby will be able to reach and grab. Don't make any assumptions about what a baby will/will not be smart enough to do. It's not a matter of smarts; it's a matter of experience, and your baby has none. These little creatures still poop themselves and laugh, so assume nothing. You never know when you might be catching an accidental twenty winks on the couch when Junior suddenly decides it is time to play with the crystal.

- **Latch your doors and cabinets:** Latches are important for the safety of your little one for many reasons. First, they keep cabinets closed so your child cannot explore the mysteries that lie within. From breakables to books, there are all kinds of things you may not want your child to test his or her strength on. Latches also prevent children who are gaining mobility from pulling themselves up and using a swing door for balance. If they lose their balance, they can hurt themselves on the corners or by hitting themselves in the head when the door swings on the hinges. Anything that is potentially poisonous to your child (e.g., household cleaners) should be moved out of reach to a higher cabinet if possible. Go ahead and latch this higher cabinet door for extra safety.
- **Keep your kid out of the toilet:** It may seem like overkill to you skeptics, but hear me out. You do not want your child to play in the toilet water for the obvious reasons of germs and water safety. A secondary benefit is that the lock will prevent your toddler from throwing foreign objects into the toilet (Mom's earrings, for example). Children's toys also have a history of causing plumbing issues.
- **Install door locks:** This is especially important if there is a room that would be difficult to childproof by its very nature, say a sewing room or home office. This is also recommended if you have a door that leads to a basement stairway. Believe me, once your

child becomes mobile, these preventative measures will become a must-have.

- **Tie up the cords to your window blinds:** These cords don't appear to be very threatening, but then again, you are not a baby. Babies have been proven to choke on these cords, or put themselves in a dangerous situation by getting them wrapped around their neck. This simple safety measure will allow you to wrap the cords out of your child's reach. Remember not to place your child's crib, playpen, etc. near an area that has these types of cords or any electrical cords that they can reach.

- **Secure your furniture:** When children are learning to become mobile, they are strengthening their leg muscles along the way. They often will look for a little help to pull themselves up, grasping anything within their reach. Unfortunately, many children have pulled over shelving units or other top-heavy furniture onto themselves, often causing various injuries. Go ahead and secure these pieces of furniture to the wall with a furniture strap that fastens to the wall, preventing the piece of furniture from toppling over onto your child.

- **Remove all glass and valuable/breakable items from reach:** The best way to really do this is to get down on all fours and crawl around your house. Anything that you can reach that is breakable needs to be moved to higher ground. This will prevent your child from injuring herself on sharp shards of a broken item.

- **Baby gate the steps:** Accidental falls are one of the leading causes of injury for both the very young and the very old. Place safety gates at the tops and bottoms of stairways in your home to prevent your baby from taking a nasty spill. You can wait to do this until your child is more mobile, but it is easier to babyproof your home all at once. You never really know when your child may surprise you by crawling off when you aren't looking. Let this be a positive moment for you instead of one where your child ends up getting hurt because you were not prepared.

It's a Fact, Baby!

What is the leading cause of accidental injury?

According to the National Business Group on Health (businessgrouphealth.org), from 1997 to 2007, accidental falls were the leading cause of accidental injury, especially for small children and the elderly. The first step to prevention in most homes is to place baby gates at the top and bottom of the stairs.

- **Use protective edges:** Places like the brick fireplace will need to be covered. Your child will want to explore once they become mobile, and hard edges like this seem to magically attract anyone under the age of ten. There are several products available that will conform to any sharp edge or corner that is potentially dangerous for your child. Performing the "crawl test" will help you identify the edges. This will prevent your child from getting poked in the eye or hurting her head.
- **Electrical outlets:** Remember the good old days, when you learned not to stick your fingers into the light sockets by, well, sticking your fingers into the light sockets? Well, times have changed. You now

need to go buy those plastic doo-hickeys and shove them into all of the unused electrical outlets for your child's safety.

- **Fire safety:** How do manufacturers ensure that your fire detector only signals that the backup battery needs changing between the hours of three and five A.M.? How do they do it? The world may never know, but along with the traditional smoke detectors, the powers that be recommend carbon monoxide detectors around the home and in your child's bedroom.

- **More fire safety:** If your child sleeps in an upstairs room, then you will want to store a fire safety ladder somewhere in the room. The ones I have seen hook right over the window and will allow you to get your child and safely climb down from the second story in case the fire in your home has progressed to a point where you cannot exit through the house. Just don't forget it is up there or your teenage daughter's sneaky boyfriend will use it as an avenue of escape.

You see, there is a lot more to do than a little light dusting and vacuuming. You want to look at your home from your baby's perspective; then you will want to go about removing or neutralizing anything that may cause harm to your child. If you aren't babyproofing your home before your child's birth, then don't wait any longer. Your child will not be giving you any warning before she becomes mobile, and you do not want to be caught off-guard. She may break something valuable to you or, worst case, sustain an injury.

First Aid

Infants require you to keep a whole host of specialty items on hand, designed especially for them. And, unlike Beyoncé only wanting green M&M's in her dressing room, these are items that may actually come in handy for your child. At home, you should keep your supplies in a baby-proof medicine cabinet, and you should also put together a travel kit for when you're running errands (yes, even to the grocery store). In these kits should be supplies that you will want on hand for day-to-day occurrences, to provide preventative health measures, and in case of minor medical situations. Here are some of the basics:

- Thermometer: There are a flood of thermometers available on the market today. The Mayo clinic (*www.mayoclinic.com*) is there for parents who need a little help. The fact is that all thermometers are not created equal. The best way to get an accurate reading is to use a digital thermometer either orally or rectally. If you want to use the rectal method, purchase a secondary thermometer for the rest of the family. Always clean thermometers after every use. The tympanic thermometer, which is placed in the ear to obtain your child's temperature, is generally accurate but can be thrown off by earwax or a smaller ear canal. The pacifier thermometers have shown to be the least accurate of the thermometer choices.
- Rubbing alcohol to clean thermometers (think airport-security size)
- Infant ibuprofen/acetaminophen
- Hydrocortisone cream
- Antibiotic ointment

- Band-Aids
- Medicine dispenser: These can come as a pacifier or bottle, or simply a plastic tube. Liquid can be placed inside to help make it easy for your child to take medicine.
- Sunscreen: Different brands and ingredients may irritate your child's skin. Ask your pediatrician or try different brands until you find one that does not irritate your child.
- Bug repellent

This should get you through the basics, and some people keep additional items for burns, rashes, splinters, and other common situations. This list won't get you through a natural disaster, but it should work to get you and your child through mosquito-infested airspace and a trip to the mall.

Emergency Supplies and What to Do

Life is full of emergencies of varying degrees of seriousness. There are the garden-variety kind of emergencies, like when you do not get your morning coffee or when your child decides he is ready for extended playtime at 4 A.M. Then there are the real emergencies where people actually get injured. Hopefully you didn't injure anyone simply because of caffeine withdrawal. So if you are in a geographical area that is prone to hurricanes, tornadoes, wildfires, etc., there are some important preparation steps you should take. This is the kind of preparation you would probably not take as a single man, figuring that you could hunt wild game on your own. But it is surely the type of preparation you will take as a responsible dad. Authorities in this arena (e.g., Red Cross) recommend that you store these items someplace that is dry and not subject to extreme temperatures. Things you should consider include:

- **Make a List:** Go ahead and make a list of everyone's contact numbers and laminate it to make it water-proof. You may have these in your cell, but what if you suddenly drop your phone while escaping the meteor that's crashing into your office? If you are like me, your child's school or daycare provider number is not memorized, just programmed into your phone, so make sure you have it available.
- **Food and Drink:** Have several days' supply of water and nonperishable food items on hand. You know, allocate a few days' worth of rations for each family member, but you don't need to go overboard and pur-chase the entire supply at your local warehouse club. However, you will need to have some baby-specific food handy and will need to periodically update any age-appropriate food that you are keeping stashed away for your child.
- **Medicine and First-Aid Kit:** You may need items to care for various minor injuries. Ibuprofen or another pain reliever should be kept in age-appropriate forms to ease any aches or fevers. If you already have a first-aid kit put together (you should!), then you should duplicate it and put it with your emergency supplies in case during a real emergency you cannot access the original kit.
- **Baby-Specific Items:** Please remember that you need to keep baby-specific items with your emer-gency supplies. Babies have their own special needs. Make sure to store age-appropriate medicine, clothes,

shoes, socks, and possibly a comfort item like a stuffed animal. This will help calm your child in case a real emergency occurs. Then make sure you update the supplies you have set aside as your child progresses in age.

The idea here is to not be caught totally off-guard if unexpected circumstances arise, so plan accordingly.

In addition to all that emergency preparation, if you have not done so yet, you, your BRP, and any family member who will spend significant amounts of time with your child should consider taking an infant CPR class. Find one in your area with a certified instructor from the American Red Cross (*www.redcross.org*) or American Heart Association (*www.heart.org*). Hey, it only costs like $25 or so, and it's just like a concert or sporting event in that watching online just isn't as good as the real thing. So get yourselves registered.

Baby Seats: Trickier Than You Think

Remember the good old days? When you would ride above the backseat in the rear window like the family cat, and go flying whenever your mom or dad had to lock up the brakes? Fortunately, someone figured out that this isn't the safest way for children to be transported. Alternative ideas like wrapping your child in bubble wrap or lining your car's interior with pillows have been tested and discarded, and for good reason: Studies discovered that infants riding in "properly installed" car seats were 71 percent more likely to survive a violent car crash, while toddlers were 54 percent more likely to survive. Today, all fifty states have their own laws that require children to ride in a car seat; each state's laws vary slightly based on the child's height, weight, and age. The general progression is: first, an infant is secured in a rear-facing infant seat. Dictated by height, weight, and age, toddlers are then put into a forward-facing car seat. And finally, your child uses a booster seat to allow the seat belt to secure them properly. Here are the newly updated guidelines for 2012 from the Governors Highway Safety Association (*www.ghsa.org*):

- All 50 states (and the District of Columbia) require child safety seats for infants and other children, depending on your state's criteria
- 48 states (and the District of Columbia) require booster seats for children who have outgrown their child safety seat, but are too small for adult seat belts
- 5 states (California, Florida, Louisiana, New Jersey, and New York) have seat belt requirements for school buses. Texas requires them on buses purchased after September 2010

Only Florida and South Dakota seem to be indifferent to the posttoddler/preteen group. But if you live in the Sunshine state or the Great Faces, Great Places state (that's the name they went with? Really?), there is nothing stopping you from going above the minimum the law requires and putting an age-appropriate booster seat in the car for your child.

So that is the low-down on keeping your kids buckled down in the car. Now the main challenge is to make sure you install the car seat correctly. Different studies have spot-checked parents' car seat installation, and anywhere from four out of ten to seven out of ten car seats have been reported as incorrectly installed. The main culprits:

- Not using the correct seat for your child's age or weight
- Not having the seat facing the correct direction
- Safety seat not correctly tightened in relation to the seat in the vehicle
- Not correctly or sufficiently tightening the safety straps onto your child
- Not making sure the seat belt fits correctly on the child when using a booster seat

Overwhelmed? Are you wondering if you have the know-how and engineering skill to safely install your child's car seat? Well, apparently you are not alone. You can actually get your child's seat inspected for correct installation. If you log on to the National Highway Traffic Safety Administration (*www.nhtsa.gov*), you can locate a local facility where they will tell you if your child's seat is installed correctly. You'll also find a link to the latest car seat recalls. Hopefully at your inspection you'll discover that you at least have the car seat facing the correct direction.

And just remember that, even if you are a remarkable driver, the roads are filled with texting, cell phone–using idiots. So while you maneuver your vehicle carefully on the roads, your (correctly) strapped-in child may get bored. It would be great if there was something you could give him to play with to help pass the time . . .

It's a Fact, Baby!

True or False: All of these safety tips, from car seats to baby gates to cabinet locks, are ridiculous!

They are ridiculous. Ridiculously effective. The CDC (Centers for Disease Control www.cdc.gov) reports that from 2000 to 2009, child death rates from unintentional accidents dropped 30 percent; death rates from motor vehicle accidents dropped 41 percent. Pass the car seat please!

Toys R You

One number that I've seen thrown around quite a bit is that it takes somewhere in the neighborhood of $200,000 to raise a child today. I am not intimately familiar with how they came up with that number, but in today's world of high-priced technical gadgetry, you could blow that amount on Christmas alone. Philosophically, it is a difficult thing to balance the perfectly natural feeling of wanting to spoil your kids and get them the best of everything with the feeling that it is absolutely reprehensible to see a sixteen-year-old driving a $50,000 car and thinking they are bad ass. (I always find myself thinking two things: 1. Your parents are the ones who are financially bad ass, and 2. How much does that insurance cost?) But that said, let's discuss the fact that you, for all intents and purposes, may be looking at opening a toy store in your home.

The child had every toy his father wanted.
—Robert C. Whitten

Where Does He Get Those Wonderful Toys?

The toy offerings available out there are as varied and expensive as ever. Why? Mainly because technology has spiraled into every part of our world, toys included. So if you are bound and determined to get Junior the red wagon you so loved as a child, just have an answer ready when he asks, "But what does it do?"

Anyway, here are a few tips on buying toys for your young child. Note: These are not tips for those who are technologically challenged; they are more safety themed.

- Keep to age-appropriate toys as labeled by the manufacturer. Just because your one-year-old is smart doesn't mean they will dive into a 1,000-piece puzzle. A look at a few of the "classic" baby toys includes:

  › **Wooden alphabet blocks:** These are fun in a few different ways for your child. You can stack them to build simple shapes and, as your child gets older, you can do some letter/sound association play with him.

  › **The "jumperoo":** As your child gets stronger and is able to hold his head up, these play sets allow your child to stand (with some assistance) and provide several toys attached to the area in his reach. Most kids really enjoy this and will soon begin to bounce up and down with their legs, helping them gain strength on the path toward learning to walk on their own (eventually).

> **Baby gym:** Let's not leave out one of the best toys for curious babies—the baby play set or gym. The younger ones lay on their backs and get to explore toys hanging down within their reach. Babies love to grab and feel the various shapes and textures of the toys and begin to explore the world around them.

- Oh, and about the puzzle mentioned previously, there's a good chance that it would end up in your child's mouth. Avoid toys with small pieces for your little one, as these are choking hazards.
- Likewise, toys with strings or cords aren't a good idea either due to the chance of strangulation.
- Toys with sharp edges are not a good idea, as babies often experiment with toys in many ways, including (accidentally) banging it on their head, eye, etc.
- It can be a good idea to sanitize or gently wash both your child's new or favorite toys. It never hurts to do a little germ prevention. This is important because your child's immune system is not fully developed, and according to WebMD (*www.webmd.com*) children are two to three times more likely to get the flu. The germs that cause the flu and colds are often transferred from one child to another when they share toys.
- Either regularly check sites like *www.recalls.gov* and the Consumer Product Safety Commission (*www.cpsc .gov*) or have alerts e-mailed to you for toy recalls (both sites allow you to sign up for e-mail alerts). Toys that have hit the stores are periodically discovered to be unsafe for one reason or another, and you don't want these unnecessarily in your child's hands.

True or False: Besides the odd malfunction here or there, children's toys are safe.

False. In 2010, nearly 10 percent of all recalls were child-related products. Make sure you or Mom has signed up to receive these notices. You can get them free via e-mail from several organizations.

That takes care of all of the general criteria of safe, age-appropriate toys. But, even after you get past the safety concerns, there are other toys that need to be avoided.

Just Say No

Through the years of parenting, you learn little tricks that both help your child play with a higher quality of toy and make sure your child does not play with a toy that will drive you absolutely bonkers. Here is a list of some of my all-timers, you know, the toys that somehow get either "misplaced," donated, or stepped on.

- **Elmo:** Yes, these are age-appropriate toys. But between "Tickle Me Elmo" and "Chicken Dance Elmo," they had to make the list. I always thought Elmo was fine as a bit player in the Sesame Street gang. Then somebody in Elmo's entourage got the idea that Elmo could go out on his own and make some real money. The result is a series of annoying dolls that do the same thing over and over. Side effects include headache, mood swings, and brain bleeding.

- **The baby doll that is a little too real:** There's almost nothing worse than the rash of baby dolls that are each more realistic than the next. The whole trend jumped the shark when someone took it too far and made a doll that you feed, and then have to change when it dirties its diaper. It's so realistic! Oh, another "realistic" thing about the doll was that it had special food that you had to buy to make this happen. Most parents don't take great joy out of changing their child's diaper. Why in the world would we buy this toy?

- **Play-Doh:** This is a sneaky one. As long as your child doesn't eat it, what's the problem? The problem is twofold: First, your child runs off and you have about thirty seconds until this stuff turns into rainbow peanut brittle. The second issue is that, inevitably, your child will decide to smash together multiple colors. While the brittle is forming, you must then frantically attempt to separate the colors, which is close to impossible due to the doughy consistency of the product. Good times!

- **Popcorn lawnmower:** This little beauty is a gift that keeps on giving! As your little child pushes the plastic two-wheel contraption forward by the handle, the mechanism inside the dome pops and the plastic balls fly and knock against the dome like popcorn, and just about as loud, but with no buttery payoff to look forward to. I wish these things had a timing belt or something that would break after a while. But no, this toy simply would not give up! One night we had to hide it away in the attic.

- **Wooden alphabet puzzle:** Just about every parent
  falls prey to this trap. It is because we think that in
  some way, shape, or form, this puzzle will help our
  child get a leg up on learning the letters and sounds
  of the alphabet. We can picture ourselves making the
  letter sounds and our little one repeating them back
  to us. Now who wouldn't want that? But for some
  reason, the shape and form of this puzzle is uniquely
  designed to cause maximum pain in a parent's foot
  when we step on the pieces, especially in a darkened
  room in the middle of the night. Somehow, this does
  not draw blood, but it actually hurts worse than an
  injury that bleeds. In addition, instead of learning the
  letters, children have been known to create a scav-
  enger hunt around the home for high-achieving parents who will not rest until they locate each and every
  letter.

- **No "off" switch:** There are toys out there—yes, I am
  looking at you, Fisher Price dog—that do not have
  an off switch. Some of these toys seem possessed, and
  will come on and talk at random times, including the
  middle of the night. They talk when they are moved
  to be put away. They seem to never stop. Parental sanity is questionable enough at times without having to
  question whether or not the stuffed dog is speaking to
  you when nobody else is looking.

- **The music studio:** Basically, this annoyance is not
  brand-specific. The toys themselves are not all that
  bad. But if your child finds something he likes, and
  all he has to do to make that likable song come on is
  push a button, chances are you are going to hear the

little tune around ten thousand times. You will find yourself humming it at work and wonder just what went wrong.

- **Sidewalk chalk:** It is a warm spring day. You decide to take your toddler out to draw pretty pictures on the sidewalk. Maybe it will be a family scene, or one with funny animals that you saw at the zoo. Whatever the picture is today, bring your Band-Aids. For this chalk will break, break, and break again until you and your child are down to a nub of chalk, certain to scrape your knuckles on the sidewalk. As you are administering first aid, you realize that you are both covered in a fine dusting of chalk powder from head to toe.

Other than that, you are on your own. I could go on, and maybe I should because this is like therapy for me. But I think you see that some toys that seem relatively harmless in the store can have unintended consequences. Just like many parenting issues, you and Mom will have your own ideas about what is correct and proper for your child. What can I tell you? You will see it all out there, including seven-year-olds with an iPhone. But that is the beautiful thing about parenting: as long as it's not harmful or neglectful, you can parent just about any way you think is right. You can chase the hot new toy, or you can only buy your child toys that do not use batteries. So enjoy, live, and learn. When you see a parent doing toy selection for his child or his naptime routine in a way that is pure genius, remember: don't panic. Just steal his ideas and make them your own.

Baby Clothes: Beyond the Onesie

Hopefully you were not the dad that looked at that three-pack of plain white Onesies and thought to himself, "This should do it until his first birthday." Dressing your child up in the cutest outfits imaginable is not something that most men think about or look forward to; however, Mom may have different ideas. Now, you may be off to a fast start when it comes to clothing your child. Maybe you had a blowout baby shower thrown for you by impossibly nice friends, who came through with tons of new clothes for your newborn. Even if this sounds like you, don't skip this section. Your baby will soon outgrow those 0–3 months clothes, and you will have to start all over again.

You may or may not get into the spirit of shopping for baby clothes, but give it a chance. You may be surprised to find yourself holding up a trendy baby jacket and asking, "Hon, what do you think?" If not, Mom might get swept up in the moment, and you may want to go along as "the voice of reason." But where do you begin? What is "recommended"? Let's start with budgetary concerns. One practical way is for you and your BRP to take a look at the budget, carve out any funds you can, and shop 'til you drop—or at least until you break a light sweat and run out of money. Another way is to find some friends and/or relatives that have older kids, and ask for hand-me-downs. Too forward for you? Have the grandparents do the dirty work. Nobody will get too offended at a new grandmother asking for donations. Finally, don't hesitate to find some consignment stores or stores offering "gently used" baby clothes. From experience, I have seen really nice stuff in these stores that looks like it was worn once at the most. Sometimes you can find off-season clothes on the cheap, so just buy that coat in the size that Junior will be next winter.

The next price point up the ladder would be to, well, to spend more money on baby clothes. You didn't think I was going to recommend extreme couponing, did you? If you find yourself in a position to do so, go ahead and build a wardrobe from the Pampers on up. If your budget is as fat as your baby's cute little thighs, there will be no end to the wardrobe additions you can find that will be nominated for "most likely to be worn once" (and only once). Just a few tips for all of your child's clothes:

- The fabrics that are difficult to care for will always be at risk of sitting in the dirty clothes pile for long periods of time.
- If you haven't discovered this yet, babies are really messy. I mean *really* messy. Remember this fact, as well as the fact that baby food and new, light-colored clothing have magnetic properties toward one another.
- Due to the facts mentioned above, your child may end up wearing multiple outfits on any given day. So in addition to "specialty" outfits, make sure to have an abundance of the basics, including pajamas. I have always felt that most adults would go out of the house in pajamas if it were socially acceptable. Why not let your child do it while they can?

If nothing else, there is a small silver lining to the baby clothes situation. As your child grows through each age range of clothing, make sure you save those old clothes. You will have options to wring a little more value out of those things. You can give them to your next child or, if your next child happens to come along and is of the opposite gender, you can donate the clothes to a charity like Goodwill (get a receipt) and use this to your advantage on your tax return. If you and your BRP decide you are done having children, then this works just as well.

Puppies and Kitties and Babies . . . Oh My!

When your child is this young, of course they will require supervision with the family pet (unless it is your goldfish, cleverly named Sushi). Young children are the most likely to contract some sort of disease from a family pet, because they are conveniently located close to the ground where all of the dirt is. Infants of course cannot walk, and lay or prop themselves up on the floor. The tendency is for babies to use their hands or mouth to explore, often picking up dirt and/ or germs when they come into contact with unclean surfaces or pets. They also have a tendency to stick their dirty hands in their mouth frequently and forget to wash their hands, because, well, they are babies. When their hands are dirty or have germs on them, it is just a really fast way to deliver the germs directly into their bodies. So if your child does inter- act with a pet, make sure both of you remember to wash up. Your child will get sick frequently enough without directly putting germs into his system. The CDC even goes as far as recommending against your child attending petting zoos or interacting with baby chicks for health reasons. I know I just ruined your Easter picture plans, but safety first! A few more tips from the 2011 American Humane Association information sheet (*www.americanhumane.org*) include:

- The AHA recommends you do a few "dry runs" by playing baby sounds in the house. They also say to get a baby doll and hold and pay attention to it like a real baby. In both cases, gauging your pet's reaction will give you a preview of how much work it will be to incorporate your baby into your existing family—animals and all.
- Try to remember that if this is your first child, there is a strong chance you will be shifting much of your attention away from your pet and to your baby. Pets have been known to get jealous of this new pecking order in the home and react poorly. On the flip side, reward your pet for a healthy reaction to the baby, or baby doll.
- If possible, try to get your pet around other children. Try to do this to desensitize your pet to children, so they can adjust more gradually.
- If your dog or cat regularly sleeps with you or snuggles in on the furniture, she may see this as her territory. When the baby comes, she may not take kindly to being demoted and act aggressively.

These are just some of the basics. I am mostly going on the American Humane Association's advice to give you an introduction to the issues you need to consider. I am still hoping to win a contest to have Cesar Milan come over and stop my dogs from pooping in the dining room. Seriously.

It's a Fact, Baby!

True or False: Your dog can make your baby sick by passing along germs to him or her.

True. Even though you are not likely to get sick by petting and playing with your dogs, they still carry germs that can cause you and your child to become sick. According to the Centers for Disease Control and Prevention, it's best to wash your and your kid's hands after touching your dog (and their slobber!).

Parental Leave

Paternity leave is a relatively new phenomenon. The basic idea used to be you knew your wife was pregnant, so you saved up all of your vacation and sick leave time. Voila! You got to spend about three weeks at home with your newborn. The Family and Medical Leave Act of 1993 helped change that. This is a summary of some of the important information from *www.FMLAonline.com*:

Created in 1993, the Family and Medical Leave Act offers employees up to 12 weeks of excused absence from their jobs every year for certain family and medical reasons. It was enacted to aid employees in balancing work and personal obligations, without having to choose between the two in times of crisis. Plus it prevents hardliner employers from firing people for taking time to be with their babies or in the case of a family medical emergency. If you have worked twelve months (and have worked at least 1,250 hours in these twelve months) or more at your company, and your company has fifty or more employees, and you live within seventy-five miles of your workplace, you are entitled to up to twelve weeks unpaid leave. The key word here is "unpaid." For financial reasons you may need to take a shorter time off. If you are a relatively new employee, make sure you double check with the appropriate authority in your office, as employers may define "twelve months" by different criteria. (Are they using your hire date, or calendar year? They are allowed a couple of different definitions under the law.) Maybe you already knew this and are on that leave right now, reading up on how to handle your newborn. If both parents are working, you can also attempt to maximize this option as used by *each* parent. This would maximize the time your child has at home with his or her parents before heading off to the world of childcare. The best way to know all of your options is to speak to the appropriate person in your workplace, usually in the Human Resources area. Use this time to build a foundation with your family. Get intimately involved in the care of your child and speed the development of the bond between you and your child. If Mom is going to be staying at home for a while, make sure you go over and above to do your part and maybe some of hers. The stay-at-home parent is a role that, seated comfortably at your quiet desk, probably does not receive enough credit from our society. The job is twenty-four hours a day. It would be great for you to experience it with no safety net (Mom) for even a few days to appreciate what it takes.

However, in today's world, more often than not Americans have transitioned to two-income families. If you and Mom are both returning to work after a predetermined amount of time, then you will need to come up with a daycare solution for your child. If this is something that your family is looking into, look for more info in Chapter 8.

Chapter 2

Crib Notes

- Make sure you thoroughly babyproof your home. Plug the electrical outlets, remove anything breakable and potentially harmful from your child's reach, pad sharp edges in the house like a fireplace, etc.
- Prepare for emergencies before they occur. Keep a first-aid kit handy at home and in your car. Keep a laminated list of important phone numbers somewhere else, say in your wallet and in your filing cabinet. This will ensure you have access to them even if your cell phone becomes disabled or broken in an emergency situation.
- Enroll in a child CPR class, and enroll anyone such as a grandparent who may spend time alone with your child. Make sure you and any other caregivers know how to apply the Heimlich to an infant. You don't want to be caught unprepared in these situations.
- Study your state's rules and regulations concerning children's safety seats. Whether you are extremely confident in your seat installation technique or not, go get it checked out at a licensed facility. You can locate the

closest one to you by logging on to the National Highway Traffic Safety Administration (*www.nhtsa.gov*).

- Try to stick to age-appropriate toys for your child. Some
  of the age recommendations are there for your child's
  safety.
- Before you go clothes shopping for your child, make
  sure you consider the household budget. Your affection
  for your child may have you going overboard!
- Your child will require supervision during interaction
  with household pets. This is especially important at
  first, as pets react differently to new playmates.

CHAPTER 3

Playing Doctor

As the saying goes, "If you don't have your health, then you don't have anything." This old chestnut applies to your baby as well. Not only do you need to keep her healthy, you need to keep her properly fed, rested, etc. But sometimes, despite your best efforts, your child will get sick. When this happens, you have only two choices: tell her to "man up," or take her to the doctor. While there is nothing wrong with a little tough love, I am going to recommend a trip to the doctor's office in this case, or at least until your baby understands what "man up" actually means. In that light, in this chapter, you'll learn all about the criteria that you should keep in mind when finding the right doctor for your baby. If you have already gone through the process and selected your doctor, then way to go! If you haven't done this yet for whatever reason (your child arrived early, you procrastinated), then soldier on. I will also attempt to provide you with information concerning the vaccination of your child. I will provide some guidance on the "where" and the "what" of a usual vaccine schedule, but you and Mom will be the ones who will have to decide the "if."

Doctor Selection for Beginners

I know what you are thinking. How are you going to help select a qualified physician for your newborn when you have not taken yourself to the doctor in years? Well, I'm here to help. Keeping your newborn healthy is kind of important after all, and in addition, the doctor you select for your child will probably be one of the most important nonfamily members in your child's life. His experience, skill, and judgment will be key in smoothing out those rough times in your child's life when she gets sick or injured. *So how do you find a good doctor?*

First you will have to define some initial criteria, such as finding a list of providers covered by your insurance and how far you are willing to drive to their office. Using a doctor outside of your health insurance plan would be really expensive, and if you utilized a doctor outside your insurance coverage, why the heck do you pay all that money for insurance anyway? So first, get that list of providers in your geographic area from your insurance company. Don't worry about the ones that might not be there; ignorance is bliss. If there is a wonderful doctor your neighbor recommends, but they aren't covered by your insurance, don't sweat it. There are usually a number of quality providers out there and most insurance directories will have each doctor's qualifications listed for you.

Second, if the option is there, you will have to decide whether you are going to see a family physician, who could treat all members of the family, or a pediatrician that specializes in children. In my humble opinion as a parent, I lean toward the pediatrician. They are on top of the ever-changing medical information as it pertains specifically to children. Many times, the medical community has modified their opinion on certain treatments for specific illnesses, and your doctor is your guide. He can help keep you informed on all the latest treatments for various ailments related to your child. I would recommend asking some questions before committing, an interview of sorts. Things you may want to ask include:

- What is your specific area of expertise/interest?
- What is your philosophy on antibiotic use? (Use them no matter what, or take the "wait and see" approach?)
- Do you return all your phone calls? (They may have a nurse call you instead.)
- Visiting the office and doing some research should help you discover if there is a "Well" and "Sick" waiting room, how courteous the staff is, the general appearance of the office, and what the office hours are. Calling to schedule an appointment, you can also ask how far out they set appointments for sick children.

Physicians come in all flavors. Some are more diagnostic experts, where they look at the various symptoms, medical history, and general health of the patient to put together the puzzle of clues to form a diagnosis. Other doctors will be more generalists, experienced in a wide variety of common children's illnesses. You will find out that each has his or her strengths and weaknesses.

It's worth mentioning that you should not join a group where you absolutely love your primary doctor for your child, but loathe his associate in the office. Invariably you will find that your child's doctor is at a conference, or on vacation, or has simply decided to work part-time going forward. Guess who will be seeing your child during those times? Correct! The doctor you decided that you do not like.

Now that we covered that little wrinkle in the doctor selection process, let's move forward. Once you have fulfilled your criteria, the next question you will need to answer is: *How does your child respond* to the doctor? How does she react when the doctor is in the room? A lot of this will go to the doctor's "bedside manner." Does he relate well to your child? Is he kind and gentle? Is your child comfortable? Does she cry uncontrollably every time the doctor comes within three feet of her? As an infant, it will be a little more difficult to tell, but as your child gets older, it will become apparent pretty quickly if your child is responding positively. Some children simply don't feel comfortable with certain doctors. Many parents have told me tales where their child simply seems to prefer a woman doctor over her male counterpart. You need to find someone that both you and your child trust because when the vomit hits the fan, you will need someone who you have great faith in telling you what needs to be done to make your child healthy again.

Although it will be painful, shop around if you have to. When your child is sick, you do not need the added stress and annoyance of knowing you have to go see the doctor you don't even like.

As a quick aside, there is one other key criteria I think is important when selecting a doctor for your child. I always ask if the doctor has any children of his own. Just like I advocate that your parenting book for men actually be written by a man, I like my pediatrician to have been through the fire himself. That way, he at least realizes when he is giving you unrealistic advice.

It's a Fact, Baby!

True or False: Babies double their weight in the first year of life.

False. The average baby will close to triple her birth weight in the first year. By the way, does this Onesie make me look fat?

Doctoral Relations

Just as it is important to gauge your child's reaction to the doctor, you will have to test him yourself. While asking some of the recommended questions listed above (plus any of your own), observe your potential doctor's response. Does he seem hurried to get on to the next patient or annoyed you have an inquiring mind? If you are made to feel like your questions aren't important or you get brushed off, it's time to find someone else. You are the one paying the bills after all.

It is also important that you feel like the doctor is doing a thorough job. If you decide to spend quite a bit of time on WebMD, your doctor should admire your thirst for knowledge rather than be annoyed by your untrained forays into the world of medicine. If you have done extensive reading on a health topic and find that the doctor is presenting ideas that contradict what you have heard, then it is okay to ask questions. If the doctor does not want to discuss or dismisses your concerns, it's time to either have an awkward conversation asking him if he is doing his job right (doctors just *love* this) or quietly move on to another provider. Quick example: I recently received an e-mail from my doctor saying no, the rumors were not true, he *did not*, in fact, have a substance abuse problem (true story). Luckily, this was my primary care physician and not my child's. I didn't really feel like digging for more information; I just called my insurance company and changed doctors. You really need to have a good comfort level and a lot of trust in these doctors. Most of the visits involve tests for ear infections or strep throat, but occasionally there will be something else going on, and you want a quality doctor who is going to know the difference between what is serious and what is not.

Playing the Percentages

When you first get to the doctor's office, you will proceed to the "Well" side of the waiting area. This will be easily determined as, on the "Sick" side, you will see kids with very visible sores and potentially vomit on the floor. I am joking here, but I always feel like a leper when I have to go on the "Sick" side, like a person who requires quarantine. Then the nice receptionist will take your insurance information, and you will be told to take your pants off and assigned a waiting area where you will wait for an extended period of time. Sorry, thinking about my upcoming physical . . .

You will have to check your e-mail and calendar quite a few times while waiting since you might be there for a while, but once you are called back from the waiting area to the patient area, your child will be measured and weighed. This is not like your doctor's visits where the scales groan when they see you coming. This is to see if your child is getting proper nutrition and is progressing properly in terms of height and weight. You will see your child get ranked in terms of percentage. You will hear something like "60th percentile in height, 50 percent in weight." This tells you where your child ranks versus infants of a similar age. So for our example, the "60th percentile in height" means that your child is taller than 59 percent of the other kids, and shorter than 40 percent of the kids. It's the same idea for weight. In boys, these tests are an early indicator of whether they are going to be the lunch money stealer or stealee. Children will have peaks and valleys due to blips on the radar like a recent growth spurt. But eventually you will see an overall pattern emerge in where your child falls on the chart. Your doctor isn't concerned about what specific range your child falls in, but rather that your child is seeing a healthy progression. Your doctor will monitor this information to look out for any unexpected hormone deficiency or genetic condition. A quick glance at you and your BRP will actually give you the best idea of how your child's growth and appearance will turn out. This is because genetics is one of the major indicators of your child's appearance.

Now, even though this is generally how your child's appointments will go, there are a bunch of different tests and visits that you'll have to focus on during your baby's first year. And when you bring your bundle of joy into the office for the first time, there will be some standard procedures that will be followed. Right from the first checkup, your doctor has a lot to cover with you and your child. The doctor has so much to cover, in fact, that we are going to dedicate a whole section to it.

1st Year Appointments

As with all things "Dude," we will speak in generalities. Don't be a stickler if your baby's one-month appointment falls thirty-two days after his birth. It takes all of the fun out of taking your baby to the doctor, if there is any fun in it in the first place. Most health professionals recommend about six or seven doctor's visits for your newborn during the first year. But this will be a time in your child's development where change and growth are happening quickly. It's important to keep donating toward your insurance deductible for the year so your doctor can monitor your child's progress and keep him healthy.

Vaccines
One way your pediatrician will work to keep your baby healthy is by keeping him up to date on his vaccines. As you may know, vaccines are traditionally shots administered by injection to give your child immunity to a specific disease or virus. Most of the vaccines are given in a form that is a dead or inactive form of the strain you are being vaccinated for, and cannot infect you. The main exception to this is the nasal spray version, which may contain a weakened form of a virus (this is not given to infants). There are many stories concerning the risks of vaccines, but on a macro level, your child is 100 times more likely to be struck by lightning than to have a severe allergic reaction to a vaccine. That being said, the choice is yours. Personally, we weighed the pros and cons and decided to vaccinate all of our children. Here is an overview of the most common vaccines:

- **HepB (Hepatitis B):** Hepatitis B is a serious condition that is caused by a virus. This virus attacks the liver leading to outcomes that can range from liver cancer, liver failure, and in extreme cases, death. The HepB vaccine is traditionally given at birth. It cannot cause your child to contract a HepB infection.
- **RV (Rotavirus):** The rotavirus vaccine protects your child from, well, rotavirus, an infection that causes severe dehydration, diarrhea, and vomiting in infants. The side effects from the rotavirus infection (as listed above) are responsible for 500,000 infant deaths worldwide. Most of these deaths occur in low-income countries where the quality of medical care is insufficient. In certain cases, such as an infant known to have a weakened immune system, the vaccine should not be given. Talk to your doctor for more information.
- **DTaP (Diphtheria, tetanus, and pertussis):** The DTaP vaccine is a three-for-one deal where, if you get the diphtheria vaccine, they throw in the tetanus and whooping cough vaccines for free. For diphtheria, the CDC says it proves fatal for 20 percent of children under five. Pertussis, or as a marketer relabeled it, whooping cough, is very contagious. It can cause severe coughing spells that prevent kids from eating, drinking, or even breathing. Nasty stuff.
- **Hib (Haemophilus influenzae type b):** The Hib vaccine protects your child from bacterial meningitis.
- **PCV (Pneumococcal conjugate vaccine):** The purpose of this vaccine is to prevent infection by the streptococcus pneumonia bacteria. It can cause meningitis (an infection of the covering of the brain),

blood infections, or pneumonia, mostly in young children. Deafness and brain damage can result from pneumococcal meningitis. This vaccine is more than 90 percent effective in preventing meningitis and severe ear infection to the children who receive it. If you pass on this vaccine, antibiotics can kill some of the bacteria later, but some calculations show that up to 40 percent of the strains are resistant.

- **IPV (Inactivated polio vaccine):** The polio vaccine has been a no-brainer ever since FDR was infected. In the interest of full disclosure, about 5 percent will experience some symptoms like cough, fever, or stomachache. Stats show that 1 percent of all people who receive the vaccine become paralyzed, so this one is scary. Polio is basically gone from America, but lingers in countries like Africa and Asia where health care standards are not as high in some areas. This is a very personal choice for parents, and I do not pretend to understand all of the science behind it. We trusted our pediatrician at the time, held our breath, and did what we believed as parents to be the best thing for our children. I respect your right to do the same.

- **Influenza:** This vaccine is only for children six months of age and older. Children under two years of age are not to receive the nasal spray version of the vaccine, which introduces live, but weakened, versions of the flu into the body. Each year a new version of the vaccine is produced to mimic what health professionals predict to be the three most common versions of the flu virus for that particular year (it changes year to year). By receiving this vaccine in an age-appropriate form, your body has the chance to build immunity to these strains before you are fully exposed to them (hopefully).

- **MMR (Measles, mumps, rubella):** This vaccine protects you from the measles, mumps, and rubella (also known as German measles). These diseases spread through the air, and are easy for your child to contract once he is exposed if he is unprotected. If your child has severe allergies or allergic reactions, speak to your doctor about it first.

- **Varicella (Chicken pox):** Chicken pox is a highly contagious virus. Patient outcomes can range from the traditional red sores and discomfort all the way up to and including death. Since 1995, when the vaccine was approved in the United States, the number of people infected and those severely affected have been on the decline.

- **HepA (Hepatitus A):** Hepatitus A is a serious liver disease caused by a virus. Twenty percent of those infected require hospitalization, and in rare cases, the virus can cause death. Children usually receive the vaccine between twelve and twenty-three months of age.

If you are not sure where you stand on the issue of having your child vaccinated, there are resources available to help you make an informed decision. Call the CDC at 1-800-232-4636 for more detailed information. The vaccines that will be given to your child during his first-year appointments are charted out in the following sections.

One-Month Doctor's Appointment: General

Now that you have done a lot of research, interviewed a ton of medical professionals, and finally selected a doctor, it is time to actually go see her. If your doctor is very popular, you may call for your baby's first appointment and receive an appointment time weeks to months away. This is okay and happens frequently. When you finally make it in, depending on how long it has been since your child's birth, he may get a round of vaccines (see following table). If this is the case, then expect your child to be sore and cranky for at least twenty-four hours. In addition, the doctor has to check on where the umbilical cord was connected to your child and see how the area is healing. The small portion of the cord left should fall off about one to two weeks after birth. Hopefully you have taken care of the area to prevent any complications such as infection. A check on the status of your child's eyesight and ear function will also be performed. Your doctor will ask questions about your child's frequency of urination and the appearance and frequency of bowel movements. No need to keep an Excel spreadsheet entitled "Baby's BM"; a general feel for consistency will do just fine.

The doctor will then look to see how your child's physical development is coming along. Doctors tend to obsessively weigh and measure children. This is mostly to check on how their growth is progressing, and partially because they need something to justify the costs. When he is weighed, the nurse will most likely require that your child strip down to his diaper. If you want to see how your baby should be shaping up month-by-month, check out the length and weight info in the next section.

Your doctor will need to know if your baby is eating formula or breastfeeding. If your baby is breastfeeding, your doctor may suggest vitamin D drops (formula has vitamin D in it). Feel free to discuss any concerns you have about your child, even including strategies to help your child sleep better during the night. And just a note: when they tell you to put your infant to bed "tired but awake," they usually forget to mention "annoyed and loudly crying" will be what comes next (read more about this in Chapter 4). Deciding how to handle this is a decision that you'll have to make with your BRP. If your child is breastfeeding, it will seem to you like the way to solve this sleeping issue will be to have Mom get up and breastfeed your child back to sleep six times a night. While this solution will leave you and the baby taken care of, Mom will suffer. So come up with a solution where both of you take on the responsibility, and both of you suffer equally. You can negotiate from there based on your individual work schedules.

One-Month Vaccines

Vaccine	Dose Number	Additional Information
HepB	dose 2 of 3	If you decided from the start to vaccinate your child, then they received their first dose of HepB at the hospital after birth. Here at the one-month visit, they usually receive the 2nd of three doses (if not, then they should at the two-month visit).

The Two-Month Doctor's Appointment

For this doctor's visit, there will be just a few changes. The length/weight measurement will be repeated, and if your child is developing any symptoms of a flat spot on his head, now is the time to do something about it. The doctor will also check your child visually and address any possible issues such as cradle cap or severe diaper rash.

Two-Month Vaccines

Vaccine	Dose Number	Additional
RV	dose 1 of 3	There are two versions of this vaccine: Rotateq and Rotarix. Please discuss which one is right for your child with your child's pediatrician. The CDC (Centers for Disease Control) states that the vaccination is 85–95 percent effective in preventing Rotavirus in children.
DTaP	dose 1 of 5	The CDC recommends that adults receive this every ten years. Are you up to date?
Hib	dose 1 of 4	Hib bacteria (*Haemophilus influenzae* type b) can cause infections in the throat or lungs that make breathing difficult. Luckily, diseases caused by Hib are vaccine preventable.

Vaccine	Dose Number	Additional
PCV	dose 1 of 4	Common reactions to this vaccine include swelling and tenderness at the vaccinated area for one in three of those vaccinated. One in three also run a low grade fever. In the rare case that your child has a severe reaction (high fever, confusion, etc.) contact your doctor immediately.
IPV	dose 1 of 4	This vaccine usually will cause soreness at the site of the vaccination. There is a low chance of serious side effects. If your child experiences any reactions that seem out of the ordinary or extreme, call your doctor immediately.

The Four-Month and Six-Month Doctor's Appointments

By now you are seeing a pattern. The doctor will want to make sure all of the basics are on schedule. This means more length, weight, eyesight, and hearing tests and questions concerning your child's sleep schedule and bathroom habits. Hopefully these things are all well and good. As parents who are probably doing a good job hovering over your baby, you will most likely notice if something is amiss.

You'll also receive more advice concerning either constipation or diarrhea, and treatment for any (hopefully) minor health issues that your baby may have (colds, etc.). At both of these appointments, your child will get another round of vaccines, most likely DTaP, Hib, polio, and rotavirus.

Four- and Six-Month Vaccines

Vaccine	Dose Number	When Given	Additional
RV	doses 2 and 3 of 3	Given at both the 4- and 6-month appts.	
DTaP	doses 2 and 3 of 5	Given at both the 4- and 6-month appts.	This schedule can seem confusing because if the 4th dose is administered after age four, then no fifth dose is needed. Your healthcare provider will help you, but you should keep track of this.
Hib	doses 2 and 3 of 4	Given at both the 4- and 6-month appts.	

Vaccine	Dose Number	When Given	Additional
PCV	doses 2 and 3 of 4	Given at both the 4- and 6-month appts.	
IPV	doses 2 and 3 of 4	Given at both the 4- and 6-month appts.	This can be administered between six and eighteen months of age. The fourth dose is administered between 4–6 years of age.
HepB	dose 3 of 3	Given at the 6-month appt.	This last dose can be administered between months 6 and 18. Please consult your doctor.

Vaccine	Dose Number	When Given	Additional
Influenza		Given at the 6-month appt.	If your child is between 6 months old and 8 years of age, then the CDC recommends that this vaccine be administered in two doses at least four weeks apart. After the first time, it is recommended annually, and will be a single dose.

It's a Fact, Baby!

Do vaccines cause autism?

No. Autism is on the rise, and symptoms often begin around the time period in a child's life when he receives vaccines. The group Autism Speaks has released a statement supporting vaccination.

Nine-Month and Twelve-Month Doctor's Appointments

These appointments have many similarities, so I've grouped them together. In addition to establishing a growth pattern, your child will possibly be finishing up a last round of vaccines depending on which type and when the cycle began. Your doctor will want to discuss and test eyesight and hearing to assure normal development. Most babies this age will sleep around 10–12 hours at night and take a nap for a couple hours during the daytime. Your child should be eating some solids at this age, and may possibly sprout some teeth. Surely, your kid's first steak is not far away! Your child should be pulling up, potentially standing, and walking. If not, don't hire a "mobility coach" just yet. The majority of children end up developing along the same arc, but they may hit certain milestones at different times. One of the huge and fun milestones you may be ready for is the start of your child talking. An exciting "Mama" or "Dada" may slip out as soon as six months, and this will gradually build to two-to-three-word sentences around 18–24 months. These are averages, so please don't panic if your child is a few weeks off these times. Just make sure you get equal coaching time to give "Dada" an equal chance of being the first word.

Twelve-Month Vaccines

Vaccine	Dose Number	When Given	Additional
Hib	dose 4 of 4	Given at the 12-month appt.	This dose can be administered anywhere between 12–18 months, according to the CDC.
PCV	dose 4 of 4	Given at the 12-month appt.	This final dose of PCV can also be given between 12–18 months.
MMR	dose 1 of 2	Given at the 12-month appt.	This is your child's first MMR. It is recommended between 12 and 18 months of age. The second dose is administered between 4 and 6 years of age.

Vaccine	Dose Number	When Given	Additional
Varicella	dose 1 of 2	Given at the 12-month appt.	As with several of the vaccines at this time, it is given between 12–18 months. The second dose is administered between 4 and 6 years of age.
HepA	dose 1 of 1	Given at the 12-month appt.	Potential mild side effects include soreness at the site of the vaccination, and headache. Severe reactions can include high fever, weakness, or breathing difficulty; immediately contact your doctor if these symptoms occur.

Note: There are really not any vaccines scheduled for the nine-month appointment unless you and your doctor decided to wait to administer one of the vaccines scheduled at six months (HepB, IPV, or Influenza).

They Grow Up So Fast

But just what constitutes fast? As we discussed in "Playing the Percentages," your child's height and weight will be put to the test when he is measured and weighed at his checkups at the doctor's office. The important thing to remember is that your baby's growth is not a contest, more of an indication of health. Your baby will usually grow in spurts, and you may notice his appetite increase around the times he is experiencing his growth spurt. There is really not a magic number for length or weight at any certain age; it's only important that your child keeps going at a steady pace. You should eventually see a pattern emerge as your child gravitates toward his target percentage.

Now, America, at its heart, is a bottom-line type of country, so I'm sure you're saying, "Enough hemming and hawing, dammit! *What* are the averages?" Well, let me tease you just a little longer with a couple "rules of thumb," averages, or guidelines that generally hold true. Babies will on average gain right around two pounds per month for the first few months. A baby can and often will double his birth weight by four to five months, and quadruple his birth weight by age two. It is pretty accurate, and helps iron out the starts and stops in growth and weight gain that are so closely scrutinized in these early months. Okay, right now there are many attorneys, CPAs, and other "type A" personalities who are ready to pull their hair out. So let us reveal some of the concrete averages that these bottom-liners are so thirsty for:

	Sex	Length	Weight
For age 3–6 months:	Boys	25.5 inches	16 lbs
	Girls	24.5 inches	14.5 lbs
For age 6–9 months:	Boys	27.5 inches	19.75 lbs
	Girls	26.75 inches	18.5 lbs
For age 9–12 months:	Boys	29.75 inches	22.5 lbs
	Girls	28.75 inches	20.5 lbs

Before you strap Junior to the stretching rack or sneak him protein shakes to beef up his stats for the scouting combine, you should know that genetics (height and weight of parents, relatives, etc.) are considered the largest influence on physical appearance, including height and weight. When two short parents have a tall child, there is often height "in the genes," meaning you can find other tall relatives somewhere in the family tree. Then again, scientists readily admit that genetics is only one of the factors that determines the final physical characteristics of people.

The important thing here is to use this chart as a guideline, and treat your child as an individual. Up until around 2000, the data on these height and weight charts were from back in 1977 and based on a limited survey of babies born in Yellow Springs, Ohio. This study was only conducted using bottle-fed Caucasian children from the 1920s to the mid-1970s. Although this sounds like something I made up, it is true. Doctors finally received more updated charts around the turn of the century. What the trends are showing is that babies are bigger in general, and kids are growing taller than in the past. The thought is that this is mainly due to the more advanced pregnancy knowledge we have obtained, the wider availability of nutritious foods, and advancements in what we now know about nutrition and the body.

Common Health Issues

In addition to all the issues that your baby's pediatrician will check for during the monthly visits—including how your baby is progressing along the weight chart—there may be other mild health concerns brewing as well. There could be some cradle cap, which can manifest itself as dry skin on the head that almost looks like dandruff, and usually (hopefully) goes away after about six months. You also need to keep that diaper fresh, or some diaper rash will develop. And if you are thinking that Junior has kind of a flat head, but shucks, he's just too cute to say anything, go ahead and speak up. Your baby could develop flat head syndrome (doctor-types call it plagiocephaly) from consistently putting pressure on one spot of your child's still hardening skull. Since the early 1990s, when doctors began recommending placing children on their back to sleep to reduce the chance of SIDS, the cases of flat head syndrome has increased almost by a factor of five. This health issue has lots of different scenarios and, in truth, is best left for your doctor to tackle. The main long-term problem with this is, well, your child will have a misshapen head! Diligence matters on this one, as the younger your child is when this condition is discovered, the easier it can be to correct due to the flexibility in your child's still-soft head.

Now there is another health issue that arises with some newborns as soon as couple of weeks after birth. If you've spotted red bumps on your precious child, there's a good chance that he could have, wait for it, "bacne." By "bacne," I am not referring to the gross version of back acne that's usually found on men; rather I am speaking to "baby acne." Yes, babies do in fact get acne, often on their cheeks, forehead, or even, yes, on their back. I bring it up here to have the ability to write the word "bacne" several times, and actually for a legitimate reason. Acne on your child that looks more like a rash or is more scaly than pimply may point to other conditions such as eczema or the aforementioned cradle cap. With parental experience you will start to have the superhuman ability to identify each of these, so don't worry if it sounds confusing.

These are some of the most common and easily fixed health problems your baby may face. There are more serious conditions and illnesses that you may encounter, and you should know a little about each to be ready if they should occur.

Illnesses

Hopefully in these early months, you will be limited to nothing more severe than skin rashes, constipation, or dehydration. These are all fairly common and treatment is quick and painless. However, if your baby has colic, I feel for you and your already ruined sleep schedule. Good luck! But as far as fighting the common illnesses like colds that babies frequently catch, here are a few tips to help keep Junior relatively germ-free:

- **Proper diet:** The majority of babies can get by just fine on either formula or breastmilk for the first four to six months. The main exception is that breastfed babies will most likely require a vitamin D supplement. As your child moves from formula or breastmilk to more solid foods, your doctor will be the best person to ask if your child needs vitamins to supplement her nutritional needs.

- **Crowd control:** This tip is actually twofold. First, keep your baby under six months old out of very crowded places, where her untested immune systems will be exposed to the general public and all of their germs. Also, keep other young children from kissing all over yours, as they may be delinquent in washing their own faces and hands.

- **Wash up:** Yet again, your mom was right. Make sure you frequently wash your hands before handling your child, and make sure that anyone else who is going to hold your child does so as well. Practice politely requesting that your mother-in-law scrub up before snuggling with your child, you know, so it doesn't come out the wrong way.

- **Play on, player:** Make sure your child gets frequent playtime and fresh air. Just like adults need exercise, making sure your child gets out and about can strengthen her little body and help her when she's fighting off a cold.

Invariably, despite your best efforts, your child will get sick. It is simply a fact of life. The hope is that she only has to deal with the less serious illnesses that are out there. When these garden-variety ones strike, it pays to know a

little about them to know when you are up against something common, or something more nefarious. Here are a few
of the semi-common illnesses your child may experience—
even though you've probably never heard of them before:

- **Respiratory syncytial virus:** This is often just called
  "RSV" and is actually more common than the flu in
  young children. It can last up to two weeks, and the
  most common symptoms are fever, runny nose, and
  a cough. Wheezing can also be an indication of RSV.
  Although you are not immune after having it, the
  effects tend to lessen with subsequent cases.
- **Hand, foot, and mouth disease:** This is an annoying condition that can spread like wildfire in a school
  or daycare. It shows up with a fever and sores or blis-
  ters on, you guessed it, the mouth, hands, and soles
  of the feet. Please do not confuse it with "foot and
  mouth" disease, which only infects livestock. It actually can also cause sores on your child's rear end, but
  finding an all-inclusive yet appropriate name must
  have become an issue at this point. This usually will
  last about a week, and isn't generally too serious.
- **Croup:** If your child starts to make sounds like a seal
  barking, then croup is the most likely cause. Croup is
  a virus that causes swelling in the larynx as well as the
  trachea. This swelling leads to the unique seal sounds
  that croup is famous for. This mostly affects children
  under six years of age, and most commonly two-year-
  olds. Severe cases can require a trip to the hospital,
  to keep your child's breathing unconstrained. It lasts
  around a week.

- **Fifth disease:** This is a yucky little virus that is more common in children than adults. It shows up usually with fever, runny nose, and headache. Yes, it does seem like all of the common childhood diseases show up that way. Joint pain may enter the picture as well. A few days into the cycle, your child will get a rash on her cheek, chest, or back (even more options, you get the idea). It was given this name by the scientist who was putting the childhood skin conditions into order and fifth disease fell, you guessed it, fifth on the list! Apparently measles, scarlet fever, rubella, and Dukes' disease all had better lobbyists.

- **Ear infections:** Ear infections are extremely common in children. The fluid buildup in your child's ear may cause pain, and your child may have reduced appetite and trouble sleeping. Antibiotics are the most common treatment. As a quick aside, if your child is about to begin daycare, just be warned. Until she builds up her immune system to handle being around so many germs, she will probably get about twenty ear infections. And you think I'm joking.

Thankfully, advances in medicine have made many of the health concerns for young children a thing of the past. Conditions like scarlet fever, whooping cough, and others are either avoided with a vaccine or are easily treatable with antibiotics.

Colic, Reflux, and Hiccups, Oh My!

Little bodies like those belonging to our babies are sometimes not running quite up to the factory specs. That is to say, sometimes there are minor problems they experience once they come off the assembly line. Colic, unfortunately, is one of those problems. In a game of "Would you rather . . ." parents of colicky babies choose the hot fireplace poker inserted into their eye every time over having to go through their child having colic again.

So what is colic? Colic is a condition in your child's digestive track that causes long bouts of uncontrolled crying. It usually presents itself within the first three weeks of your child's life and, unfortunately, its cause or causes remain shrouded in mystery. Sound a little vague? Well, to add to the frustration of this illness, there is really not a single consistent cause of colic, just educated theories. The best theories are that there is a problem in the child's digestive system that doesn't allow for normal digestion. This causes bloating, gas pains, and intestinal pains in your child. In turn, he cries. A lot. These periods of crying often interfere with the baby's sleep schedule, causing further distress and more crying. This doesn't make things easy on you either, and neither you, your BRP, nor your baby's favorite blanket has the power to console him.

There is some evidence that overstimulation of a colicky child will possibly agitate the condition, as will overfeeding or any number of other causes. As we noted, there really is not a single defined cause, but doctors know it when they see it. The only saving grace to the condition is that your child's body will usually take matters into its own hands and heal itself. Most children will outgrow the condition by three to four months of age. So find that super kind grandparent who is a glutton for punishment, and take a night to yourselves.

It's a Fact, Baby!

Who is better at changing diapers, men or women?

Men! A study showed that men clocked in a faster average time to change their child's diaper. So whether it's
our large, rippling muscles that allow for this, or our
pretending we are part of a NASCAR pit crew, it is one
area we can claim victory in the battle of the sexes.
The bad news is that our reward is changing all of the
diapers.

Vision and Hearing

In simpler times, like say, the 1980s, we didn't seem to know
a lot about the world around us. Sane-minded people still
smoked; corporations cared about their employees; and nobody
thought much about the growing cloud of black smog that
appeared above large metropolitan areas. Likewise, we didn't
seem to know a whole lot about what babies could actually see
and hear. We just kind of took it all in stride. In today's world
of "no stone unturned" and a definitive answer to every question in less than three seconds, much more has been learned.
But when it comes to vision and hearing problems, outward
symptoms are subtle. We will cover the most common indicators of a hearing or vision issue with your child.

Vision
Gone are the days when doctors and parents alike
thought babies could only see clearly seven to ten inches in
front of their faces. Today we know that a baby's eyes exit the
womb ready for action, with all of the parts working and the

ability to focus on objects of any distance. But for the first two months or so, your child is still perfecting her focusing talents, so her vision might not be as crystal clear as that of an adult.

It's a Fact, Baby!

True or False: Sitting too close to the TV or computer screen will damage your child's eyesight.

False. Although too much TV isn't great for learning, it doesn't damage children's eyes.

Brain development also plays a role in your baby's eyesight. Although a baby's eye is working close to perfectly, and all the equipment is there, the portion of her brain that translates the image is not quite developed enough yet. A couple of studies have been done and in effect, a newborn might have something comparable to 20/120 vision. By four months old, this has improved to something in the neighborhood of 20/60 vision, and by eight months of age, we have gotten to 20/30, very close to regular adult vision.

As for other common questions that you may have, here are the highlights. Yes, babies as young as two weeks of age can distinguish between colors, although at that young age subtle shades of the same color may cause some difficulty. No, there does not seem to be any one color that is "right" to use in your child's room (or playroom); they are interested and stimulated by them all. Finally, a little research shows that your baby probably recognizes your face somewhere around three months of age, but recognizes the sound of your voice much earlier.

The most outward signs you may keep, um, a lookout for include:

- **Unequal Pupils:** This may be the sign of nerve damage or a tumor
- **Consistent Tilt of the Head:** This has been shown to be a sign that your child is having blurred or double vision
- **Damaged Pupils:** If part of the iris is missing, it is an indicator of an eye defect

Keep your eyes peeled for these symptoms, and read up on more at *www.childrenseyefoundation.org*.

Hearing

As for your child's hearing, there are some similarities to the way your child's vision works. Babies hear fairly well, but not perfectly due to the fluid from the birth process that remains in your child's middle ear, which is perfectly normal. Also preventing your child from hearing you sneak in and check on her in the middle of the night is the fact that parts of the ear are not fully developed at birth. It is due to these factors that babies respond best to higher-pitched and silly "baby talk." So put your manly pride to the side, get in front of the mirror, and practice those ridiculous antics that both infants and those around you will find so amusing.

You may not have noticed it in all of the chaos, but most hospitals test babies' hearing before they leave the hospital.

The most outward sign of a hearing issue is if your infant does not respond to sudden loud sounds that occur close to them. Also, if they do not respond to your voice unless you speak quite loudly, they may have a hearing issue. Please mention this to your doctor at your appointment, or even set an additional checkup for this issue if you are very concerned. Despite the myth, most hearing problems are not caused by a earwax buildup in your child's ear. But, that doesn't mean you can allow your child to become unwashed. Which brings us to the topic of . . .

Hygiene

Babies do not seem like they would require much hygienic upkeep. They do not have much hair, don't sweat, and don't have any teeth. But, since they get food and slobber on everything, they still have to be bathed. You are helping give your little slugger or ballerina a bath, aren't you? You can put his little tub in the kitchen sink, and wash him right after you take care of the dishes. Just remember not to throw the baby out with the bathwater . . . sorry, it had to be said; I wanted to think of a scenario where that saying actually applied. If you are a semi-successful individual, I think you understand the basics, but it doesn't hurt to review. His care routine looks a lot like yours, only without the razor, Rogaine, and excessive hair gel. So what are the major hygiene issues that infants face? Let's get down and dirty with a list of baby hygiene issues:

- **Bathing:** For the first week or two, you will want to gently wash your child with warm water and a washcloth. Continue this until any remaining umbilical cord falls away. Then you will want to bathe your child probably once or twice a week with a gentle, chemical-free soap and warm water. Once your child gains mobility, he will be scooting on the floor more often, picking up dirt and requiring more frequent bathing.

- **Skin Care:** Your child has the cutest little skin. Unfortunately for wintertime, both cold outdoor air and indoor heat can dry your child's skin, leaving it dry and itchy. In the summer, the sun, chlorine, air conditioning, and salt water can dry out his skin. This means whether you go to the beach or pool, you will have to take care year round. Reduce bath times to around ten or fifteen minutes, and do all of the washing at the end so your child is not sitting in soapy water, which dries out the natural oil of his skin. Apply moisturizer liberally to his damp skin after the bath. Bubble baths also dry out the natural oil of his skin, so limit these to special occasions. If liberal application of moisturizer does not seem to be doing enough, run a humidifier in the rooms where your child spends the most time. If your child develops itchy, red patches on his skin, he may be developing a skin condition called eczema. By itself, eczema is not enough to load up the car and head to the doctor's office. But if the area persists or continues to spread, make sure to bring it to your doctor's attention and let her decide the best treatment.

- **Baby Skin and the Great Outdoors:** In addition to dry skin issues, you will want to protect your child from the outdoor elements. In the winter months, this mostly consists of the appropriate clothing for the temperature. In the summer, it is best to keep your child in the shade and out of direct sunlight as much as possible. Lightweight clothing including long sleeves and a hat can be utilized to keep the sun off your child's skin as well. Pediatric dermatologists have stated that sunscreen is safe for your baby's skin, but they recommend the versions made with either zinc oxide or titanium oxide, which simply form a barrier on your skin, preventing sun damage. Other sunscreens are made with chemicals, which are absorbed into your child's skin. Doctors are unsure what effect this may have on your child's skin long-term, hence their preference.

- **Finger and Toe Nails:** Your child may accidentally scratch himself if he grows long fingernails and toenails. You should trim his fingernails about once (or more) per week. Toenails grow more slowly, so they require less trimming. It is an old parents' trick to perform this nail maintenance while your child is distracted by another parent, or even asleep if possible. This will allow you to trim with the least chance of accidentally clipping too close to his fingers and toes.

As you've probably noticed, there is a lot of care and maintenance happening with your child. All the while, you need to train yourself to notice what is "normal" and what signs may indicate an issue that requires more investigation. Don't worry; it gets easier with time.

Chapter 3

Crib Notes

- Selecting a doctor for your child is extremely important. Make sure your child responds positively to the doctor. It's also important that you feel as though the doctor is ready and willing to spend time with you to address any concerns you are having.
- Getting your child vaccinated is an important decision. If you are not going to, make sure you are making an educated choice.
- Your child's height and weight percentages are not really as important as a pattern of steady, healthy development.
- Your child will most likely grow in fits and spurts, and have an increase in appetite when these growth spurts occur.
- Modern medicine has eliminated some of the more serious medical conditions for children. There are still a few—like croup; hand, foot, and mouth; and RSV—that you need to be aware of.
- Your child's eyes are not fully developed at birth, but by eight months old they can see almost as well as adults.

- Babies are often born with some fluid in their ears and can hear high-pitched voices more clearly.
- Address your child's hygiene on a regular basis. A regular bathing schedule is a good first step.

CHAPTER 4

Eat, Sleep, Poop, and Other Exciting Things Babies Do

Babies are like you, only cuter and more helpless. And since babies do not exit the womb ready to wolf down double cheeseburgers, you will have to decide how and what they are going to eat. You will also need to care for and comfort your child as he figures out the whole sleeping routine. Then there is the whole changing of diapers and potty training. In good time babies will develop into full-fledged people, hopefully happy and productive ones (cross your fingers), that know how to use the toilet. Because once that cuteness fades, there aren't many people around who are willing to change your diaper. In addition, your child's vocal abilities will be picking up, so we will look at how that beautiful duet (or even a round!) may go. Keep your eyes open! Your child will soon be gaining mobility and you don't want to miss a moment. You also do not want to let your child out of your sight, as he is prone to injure himself. Finally, we will take a look at teaching your child some sign language (yes, I'm for real right now). If I did it, then you certainly can if you choose.

Feeding (Months 1–3)

When it comes to feeding your infant, first you must make a decision: breast or bottle? While we know which you prefer, Dad, you sly dog, what we will be discussing at this juncture is less riveting but more important: will your child be breastfed or drink formula from the bottle? The executive summary of this section is as follows: Breastmilk is superior for many reasons, but many a baby has been raised on formula and turned out just fine. Also, babies tend to eat about 6–8 times daily, so you and Mom are going to spend a lot of time feeding your child.

Breast in Show

If you still, um, thirst for more knowledge on this subject, want to be bottle-fed all of the reasons why breastmilk is better, or perhaps are simply enjoying the material so much that you just cannot stop yourself from reading on, we will milk this topic for all it's worth. The body is pretty cool, and I would probably have liked to study medicine if I wasn't burdened with "LGS," otherwise known as "Low GPA Syndrome." Anyway, in this case we will look at the breast with amazement at what it can do.

Your BRP's brain recognizes what your child will need and starts telling Mom's body to produce colostrum, a substance almost yellow in color and thicker than breastmilk. Colostrum would be the first food for your breastfeeding child, and it contains a high concentration of extremely nutritious antibodies; it's also easier for your child to digest than formula, helps prevent jaundice, and acts as a laxative to help your child with his first bowel movement. The colostrum production lasts for a few weeks.

Your BRP's body then sends out the word to get the breastmilk flowing. Again, amazingly the body subtly alters the exact composition of the breastmilk at any given point to give your child just the right amount of nutrients that he needs. The minerals in breastmilk are more efficiently absorbed by your child, and in turn produce less waste, which is of interest mainly because you are on the waste disposal team. Finally, breastmilk is probably better for brain development, although by what degree I cannot find anyone willing to say. What doctors do agree on is that breastmilk is basically the ideal composition for a baby.

Breastfeeding can be a double-edged sword for you, Dad. You will not be as involved in the feeding process for obvious reasons. This will limit you from a major bonding moment with your child. Also, Mom will at some point feel she is "on call" day and night to feed, and naturally become frustrated and feel a little trapped (you would to). But there are times when your breastfed baby will want to be fed and Mom will not be available (work, sleep, etc.). So for when these circumstances arise, the breast pump was invented.

The Breast Pump

No, I haven't lost my way and decided to give you a recommendation out of the Kama Sutra. The breast pump is a handy, if slightly unnerving, device that will allow your BRP to extract the breastmilk from her body and place it into bottles for later use. "Why is it unnerving?" you may be asking. I personally found it a little weird that this machine was pulling milk out of my wife while issuing Darth Vader–like sounds in perfect rhythm like a metronome. Maybe I'm the only one, but I figured I'd warn you. But, no matter how unnerving it may be, the breast pump gives your family more feeding flexibility and allows you to participate in nighttime feeding even if you decide to only feed your child breastmilk. Also, working mothers often pump their milk during the work day for the person caring for their child to use. Although I suspect milk collection at the workplace for women is as much fun as infertility testing for men (see *Dude, You're Gonna Be a Dad!* for further explanation), it will allow Mom to work and still keep your child on breastmilk. The main issue with this magic cure-all called the breast pump is that it can run between $200–$300. All of those formula savings down the drain! But all is not lost. Contact your insurance carrier to see if your plan will help pay for the purchase of the pump. Some of them may only do so under certain conditions, like if your doctor deems it medically necessary. There are so many variables here, I can only cross my fingers and point you to the phone to contact your insurance carrier.

Formula-Fed

As for formula, it is nutritious and contains many organic compounds that are helpful for digestion. Most health organizations still certify breastmilk as the best choice, but formula is a healthy alternative. There are natural compounds contained in breastmilk that are not in formula, and Mom's body will actually change the makeup of the breastmilk to help give the baby exactly what he needs. Formula simply cannot match this! But formula has benefits also. One of these benefits is that formula can allow you to get more involved in the feedings, including in the middle of the night. Yes, you can be a willing and able assistant to feed pumped breastmilk to your child, but Mom will still be feeding your child directly fairly often. With formula, you can be part of the process, bonding any and every time if you choose. Formula-fed babies need to eat less often, as the formula is more difficult to digest and sticks around longer. This may translate to more consecutive hours of sleeping at night, which is great. The con is that formula is more expensive, as breastmilk costs, well, nothing.

What, you *still* haven't skipped ahead yet? You are parched for even more knowledge concerning breastmilk and baby formula? Well, just as a baby receives "hindmilk," or breastmilk higher in fat content, at the end of a breast-feeding session that helps them to feel full and ease into a nap, we are done here, and will now ease our way over into the world of infants and how they sleep.

It's a Fact, Baby!

True or False: Most babies cry two hours per day.

True. When you add up the little minutes here and there, most young babies cry about two hours per day. When the amount of crying was measured, the highest amount of crying per day occurs when babies are about six weeks old, and it then decreases as the baby reaches around three months old.

Sleeping (Months 1–3)

Do you know all about your circadian rhythms and melatonin production? If you travel across time zones on a regular basis, you probably do. Basically, light and darkness cue your body's master clock when to produce melatonin, a naturally occurring hormone in the body, which makes you drowsier and ready to get to bed for the night. Newborns' bodies are like the guys from *The Hangover* movies, and they don't quite know if it's day or night, which means that it takes a while for them to develop the traditional day/night schedule. You will quickly learn this when, as your child is taking a marathon nap during the day, you are enjoying the peace and quiet, tiptoeing around the house, making yourself an ice cream sundae, and taking a short nap. Later that night, as Leslie Nielsen once exclaimed, the "cows will come home to roost." The long daytime nap will have Junior rocking and rolling in the 3 A.M. time slot. Let's hope it's Mom's night with the baby (just kidding, I would never engage in guerilla warfare like that).

It's a Fact, Baby!

True or False: Babies smile while they are asleep.

True! Babies smile while they are asleep right from birth. While doctors often like to remind us that there is no emotional content to their smile during sleep, I prefer to think of them having dreams of puppies and bunnies.

The good news is that, sometime around three months, your child will start to get the hang of this whole "light = wakey time and darkness = sleepy time" thing. This is due to the development of a baby's brain. Depending on your child's rate of development, around month three his brain develops enough to allow for a more regular sleep schedule, instead of napping in 1–2 hour blocks throughout the day and night. In addition, near month three, your child's stomach will grow and he will be able to hold more food in there.

In turn, he can stay fuller longer and rest for longer periods. The thing to remember is that there is not a "magic" way to get your child to sleep more during the night. Each child is totally different, and even siblings can vary wildly on when and how they settle into a civilized sleep schedule. If you are trying to let your child "cry it out" before he is old enough to develop a sleep pattern, then you are probably just wasting your time.

Sleeping Safely

As for safety, newborns up until the age of one are at risk for SIDS, or Sudden Infant Death Syndrome. Scary stuff. Scarier still, in today's age of medical marvels, doctors still do not know exactly what causes it. However, they have been able to identify risk factors which include:

- Blankets or toys in the crib
- Co-sleeping (baby sleeping in the parents' bed)
- Being around cigarette smoke in the womb or after birth

In addition, you want to make sure you're following the #1 rule: ALWAYS PUT A BABY TO SLEEP ON ITS BACK. Sleeping on their stomach increases the risk of SIDS, and putting them to sleep on their side increases the possibility they will roll onto their stomach while asleep. Personally, I decided as a first-time dad that I would just stay up and listen to my baby breathe until her first birthday. Turns out this isn't possible. But if you went to check on your child in the middle of the night, you wouldn't be the first or last to do so.

To Cry or Not to Cry

Let's wade into less choppy water concerning another sleep issue. This is the debate about what you should do when you hear your baby crying after you have put her in bed, or at some point during the night. There are two schools of thought on the topic, being A) rush into the room and comfort/rock her back to sleep or B) take the more Spartan approach and let her "cry it out." Most doctors recommend that going through all kinds of lengthy and complicated bedtime routines like a bath, rocking and singing of multiple songs, and a reading of *War and Peace* (or at least two out of three of these) will encourage your child to expect this. As she gets older, she will only be able to sleep if you perform the routine and put her to bed almost totally asleep. But there should be a short, simple bedtime routine, such as reading a single story to your child, to let your child and your child's body know that bedtime is coming and she needs to wind down. Then, as the doctors say, around four months of age you should, at least once daily, lay her down to sleep semi-drowsy, but awake. The only problem I have personally experienced with this theory is when you lay your child down to sleep, as recommended, drowsy but awake, they don't ever *go to sleep*. You feel foolish dutifully listening in the monitor while your child lies awake for an hour, gurgling, crying, and occasionally cooing. Perhaps we didn't stick with the plan, but believe me, we tried. So my note of caution would be to do what works best for you and your family.

Having a child is surely the most beautifully irrational

act that two people in love can commit.

—Bill Cosby

Poop Goes the Weasel

In this play-on-words of the title of a nursery rhyme, your child is the weasel. Oh, and he will poop. I even found one doctor who told me that anywhere from one "up to fifteen" poops per day may be considered normal. Boy do I feel sorry for those parents whose children fall on the upper end of *that* scale! But when it comes to this particular topic, it seems to me the most important thing is for you to know what's normal, and what's not . . .

What's Normal?

- Slightly straining, grunting, or face turning red is completely normal.
- In the first weeks, you should see green-brown coloration, with some liquidity.
- At about one month, breastfed babies will then produce orange-brown stool with what one doctor describes as a "sweet and sour" smell. If he says so!
- Formula-fed children go right to big, bad Leroy Brown stools that are generally more solid than those of breastfed babies.

What's Not?

- Diarrhea is a real problem for infants. If you are unsure, this would be complete liquidity with a stronger smell. Believe me, you will know it. Babies can become dehydrated, and persistent diarrhea coupled with fever and excessive crying should lead you right to the doctor's office.

- Constipation is the flip side to the same coin. This is usually observed by extremely dry stool, and your child may even cry while the stool exits the body.
- Any signs of blood in stool or urine are abnormal, and you should take your child to the doctor right away.

Well, that was a fun topic. I tried to make it through in a mature, efficient manner. I had all of these wonderful terms for pooping, including eliminate, waste production, dropping the kids off at the pool, and good old "number two." It seemed a shame to finish off this topic without mentioning them.

It's a Fact, Baby!

Most parents feel they have changed a million diapers in their lifetime. Care to hazard a guess at the actual number?

By the end of the first two years, the average baby has had about 7,300 diaper changes.

Talking and Signing

Talking to your child is pretty natural. Singing to your child, for us nonmusicians, is probably a less natural way to interact with Junior. But this kind of one-on-one interaction is actually very important for his intellectual, emotional, and social skill development.

Your child goes through rapid growth in his ability to communicate with those around him from birth to three years of age. He learns from those who are around him the most, probably you and your BRP. The one-sided conversations will help him grasp (on a baby level) the rhythm and patterns that are part of conversation. These are things we don't even think of, but they are important for your child to be exposed to. Do you know what else these sometimes silly conversations can do? They may help you bond with your child and will help you begin the process of incorporating your new family member into your life. The good news is all you have to do is talk to your child. It doesn't matter if he can understand you or not.

Do you know what else is really cool? Teaching your child sign language. I know, it sounds kind of far-fetched and a little like starting a compost pile in your backyard. (I was counted among the skeptics.) But study after study (and my youngest daughter) have proven that you can begin teaching your child to sign at ages as young as two to three months (WebMD says start at six months), and that most kids will start signing back to you at somewhere around six to eight months of age. The ages of both when you start signing to and in front of your child as well as when they are able to sign back to you coincide with development of certain cognitive and motor skills. As with so many skills, each child will develop at a different pace, and with different levels of ability. But even if you do not start right away, that doesn't mean it's too late. The key words to remember when working with your child on signing skills are patience and repetition. A few other keys to signing with your child:

- Focus on teaching him practical signs that he can use, such as "Mommy," "food," "milk," "more," etc.
- Try to get any other caregivers such as grandparents to reinforce the signs as much as possible.

- Remember that teaching your child to sign takes patience.

A good start to this process is to either research the common signs you want to teach your child on the web or purchase signing flash cards. This is not only a way to bond with your child, it is a way to begin communicating with him earlier than if you wait until he learns to talk. On that subject, it has been proven signing does not delay speech development, so that should not concern you. This is a fun and unique little project for you and your child. I was a nonbeliever, and my wife did most of the practice with our child. But I was amazed as our daughter began to sign "more" and then "done" one day while eating. It was amazing!

Chapter 4

Crib Notes

- Infants are growing and changing all the time. They need nourishment to keep growing, so on average an infant may feed six to eight times a day.
- Many reasons, mostly because of the amazing things our bodies are capable of, make breastmilk superior to formula. However, if you do feed formula to your child, it is a worthy substitute.
- The mother's body naturally makes subtle changes to the composition of the breastmilk, depending on what your child needs.
- Breast pumps are very useful tools for breastfeeding mothers who cannot be with their child all day. It will allow you to have the bonding experience of feeding your child if you have not done so.
- At about three months of age, your baby will begin to develop a firm sleep schedule. Change it at your own risk!
- Always put your child to sleep on its back. This is the *number one* rule to help avoid SIDS.

- You will become an expert on the subject of your child's poop. Make sure to know what's normal and what could represent a problem with your child's health.
- Infants can be taught to express themselves through sign language. It really helps them communicate with you, and it helps you know what they want.

PART 2

Months 4–7

Are you feeling "the burn" yet? By "the burn" I mean the mental and physical toll of having a newborn baby in the house to care for. You're tired all of the time, and so is Mom. You may be experiencing what is unofficially called "baby brain," where you feel like you're not quite firing on all cylinders. In this Part, we are going to take you and your semi-functioning brain through months 4–7 of your child's development. You will get to peek into one of the major challenges of parenting: once you think you are getting things down pat, the game changes on you. Coming soon to a living room near you, your child will begin to show signs of mobility. That's a game-changer. The first time you are diligently putting away clean dishes and turn around to find that your child has moved, your heart will stop for a second. Then you will have to watch them even more closely, as babies are a curious sort and will want to explore. They like to get a handle on everything and anything, because it is all new to them. Get ready for more growth and change—all discussed here—as you enter the next stage of your baby's development.

CHAPTER 5

Babies Grow Like Weeds

Babies are constantly growing and developing. They are focusing right now on their motor skills, while also physically developing, rolling over, and sitting up. They will now sort of respond to your rhetorical question with a "coo" that is cute and funny all rolled into one syllable. You cannot stop these kids; heck, you can only hope to contain them. During months 4–7, you will also continue to take your little one in to the doctor to ensure that your child's rapid development stays on the proper course. As your child's development continues, your child will be learning and showing off his new talents all of the time. In addition, as he continues to grow and change, we will discuss his evolving sleeping habits. Ouch! Something just bit me! It may be that your child will begin teething, and we will take a look at that as well. This is also an exciting time for everyone, as your child will take note of your excitement when he does something new. It is a fun time to bond together as a family.

Medical Considerations:
The Four-Month and Six-Month Medical Issues

We have covered the doctor's appointments in the first year of your baby's life in Chapter 3, but we didn't discuss all the things going on with your baby. Let's look at some of the cool medical-related stuff going on with your child at this stage.

- **Lady Antibodies:** This does not refer to antibodies with a southern or country flair like a certain popular country band. At birth your child's body comes complete with one type of sickness-fighting antibody—Immunoglobulin G (IgG), which fights against both viral and bacterial infections—that he developed in the womb. That's good, because right after you have a child no one wants to go out and buy antibodies. Kidding of course (but trust me, you're really not going to want to run out to get *anything* with a brand new baby at home), but these antibodies begin to fade away around the fourth month, and your child's brand new immune system starts to take over. If your child is breastfeeding, then he will still receive some antibody support from your BRP, but it is at this point that you will see babies potentially begin to catch colds, especially if they have older siblings or begin daycare. Keeping their hands and toys as clean as possible may help, but there are so many ways for your baby to be exposed to germs that you may just have to do what you can and know that your baby will probably get sick at some point anyway. Don't worry, it happens to everyone.

- **Weight for It:** Your baby's fat percentage will usually increase around this age in preparation for more growth down the line. The brain is made up of about 50 percent fat, and during his first year, your child's brain will as much as triple in size. His body will use the fat from the foods he eats to fuel this growth.
- **Motorhead:** No, your child will not necessarily enjoy this heavy metal group's music. But his motor skills will be showing signs of progress. Your child will grab at almost anything that comes into his reach. This includes hair, neckties, and necklaces, so watch out!

But now we are getting to some of the child's first exciting signposts along the way to the biggies, like first steps. They might be doing little baby pushups, and they may begin to roll over. Be careful though. As exciting as this is, once your baby begins to gain mobility, it will be the end of putting him on a blanket on the floor and watching TV. Somewhere in here your child will begin teething, and probably sticking anything he can get his hands on into his mouth.

It's a Fact, Baby!

True or False: Less than half of all mothers go back to work within six months of giving birth.

False. According to the most recent figures published in 2010, 55 percent of mothers are back at work within six to twelve months of giving birth.

Physical Growth and Development

Your child is getting bigger and, at the same time, he is developing skills. They may not be very marketable skills in the workplace, but you have to start somewhere. Let's take a look at some of the highlights:

- **Rolling both ways:** No more of that "only rolling to the left" stuff, mister! If your baby only seems to want to roll to one side, it is normal, and in a little time he will figure out rolling in the opposite direction. It's time to bite the bullet and roll left *and* right. This is a sign of growing strength and muscle coordination.
- **Playing hide and seek:** Your child is learning that objects exist outside his field of vision, which, if you like to name drop, is referred to as permanence. It shows that your baby's brain is developing and understanding more complex ideas.
- **Sitting without support:** You may want to put some pillows around your baby at first, but around this time your child's muscles will strengthen to allow him to sit upright.
- **Vanity:** Just kidding. Your child will love to look at his reflection in the mirror, but most experts state that your child doesn't realize he is looking at himself. It is theorized that babies like mirrors so much because they think they are playing a "copycat" game with another baby!
- **Stand and deliver:** The first time you turn around and see your child standing up, it will freak you out. He probably cannot stand by himself quite yet

(most babies can pull themselves to standing position around eight months of age), but he will be able to with your help to balance him. For some reason, at this age babies like to bounce up and down . . . probably in an attempt to exhaust you and get what they want.

- **Respond to you:** Around this age when you are carrying on those silly but fun one-sided conversations with your child (Should we get the Bud Light or Miller Light? What do you think?), your child will begin to respond with sounds of his own. Just don't expect them to make much sense.

- **Bablyon 5:** Yeah, your child is going to be making all kinds of sounds. Most of them will involve a string of letters like somebody mashed his hands on your keyboard, and unless you are a member of the Psi Corps, you will never know their intended meaning. It's still extremely cute, and it's the first step to your baby learning real words. And while we are discussing your child's mouth . . .

It's a Fact, Baby!

What part of your baby's body accounts for about one-quarter of his body weight?

Your baby's head. Your child's body will eventually become more proportionate, but for now get used to your child having a disproportionately large (but cute!) head.

These Things Have Teeth?

Well, when they are born, they don't of course. The majority of children start getting teeth somewhere around the six-months age marker. Signs that your child might be teething are about the same way you feel when you wake up Monday mornings for work—crankiness and excessive drooling. The symptoms can start before you see teeth, so be forewarned. Little known fact (at least in the man community): babies get their teeth in pairs, beginning with the two bottom teeth (right in the middle). Yes, you pesky nags, this isn't true of *every* child, but it's the general pattern. Your child may begin to chew toys and anything else he can when teething occurs, to help relieve the pressure he is feeling. He may also tug at his ears as the pain and pressure move up toward the ear canal.

It's a Fact, Baby!

Babies are born with tiny buds of teeth inside their gums, and yes, occasionally some babies are born with a tooth or two. But what body part are babies born without?

Kneecaps! Almost all babies are born without kneecaps, which do not develop until the area ossifies around age two or three.

In case you don't remember, teething actually causes some pain or discomfort. If it becomes a problem for Junior, then you can give him a cold teething ring, or some parents will administer infant ibuprofen (remember not to give babies under six months of age ibuprofen without your doctor's permission). I think most parents outside of the boonies know better, but don't try rubbing a little alcohol on your baby's gums; it's simply unhealthy. The other idea that often comes up, but is unsafe, is to give them something like a frozen carrot or banana. At the average teething age, these could quickly become a choking hazard and should be avoided. Until those pearly whites come in, you can perform some oral hygiene for your child by taking a clean wet washcloth and wiping your child's gums twice a day to help prevent bacteria from building up. When the teeth actually arrive, you can just gently brush them without toothpaste, until age one, when a pea-sized amount of nonfluoride toothpaste can be used. This will get your child started down the road to healthy teeth and gums.

Mobility

Parenting has some interesting dynamics to it. You enthusiastically celebrate every milestone and sign of progress your child makes, and rightfully so. At the same time, with each new stage reached, your life as a parent becomes more complicated. Your baby gaining self-powered mobility is no different.

Somewhere around six months in, you are probably feeling like you have a good routine established. Between your baby's nap schedule, and the fact that you can just put your child on a blanket with a few toys and know that he can't wander off, he is fine as long as you are in the area. Up until now you have had the ability to try to get a few things done on your "master list," or catch a few minutes of your favorite show, cleaning up the backlog on the DVR. Then, partway through *The Amazing Race*, you look over and see that your child has moved from the spot you placed him on and panic, and a whole new stage of parenting ensues as you begin your own amazing race to find your baby.

Now that he can begin crawling (usually around seven months), you are going to be on the move quite a bit as well. Now, instead of your child pointing or verbalizing if he sees an object he would like to examine, he becomes inclined to just make a break for it so he can check things out for himself. Now that your child is mobile, you will receive feedback on how well you have babyproofed your house (as we went over in Chapter 2). If you forgot to move the glass figurine grandma gave you, your child will find it for you. Many parents choose to use a baby gate to block off the top and bottom of the stairs to prevent a fall. Also, resist giving your child baby walkers with wheels. There is no proof that he will learn to walk more quickly, and this crutch allows him to go places that may be unsafe. Plus, your baby just doesn't have great control yet and may be prone to spills and running into objects that may injure him.

The most common reason babies are late developing mobility is that they are constantly held, and not given a chance to properly develop the strength to get themselves moving. The lack of use of your child's muscles may cause the muscles to strengthen at a slower rate, and your child won't gain the muscle coordination required to get up and go all by himself. So allow your baby time to play on the floor and use his muscles, which will aid in his development. Also, make sure that you and your BRP communicate as to who is keeping an eye on Junior. You don't want to think each other is running point on this duty, only to find out that neither parent is watching your newly mobile child!

Eating and Nutrition

Between 4–6 months is when the American Academy of Pediatrics recommends you introduce solids, as your child's digestive system should be developed enough to process the food and extract the required nutrients. But, how do you know when it is the right time? The more likely process is when one of the parents decides it is time to introduce some solid food, or when your child makes a grab at something on your plate and you spontaneously decide to let him have a little nibble just to see what happens. Here are a few things you should consider before you throw a half rack of ribs on Junior's plate:

- Your child will need to be strong enough to hold his head upright. He needs good head and neck control to eat solids.
- Interested? You will see your child reaching for your food, or staring down your plate, as if to say, "Hey mister, slide that thing over here."

When you decide to start introducing solids, don't think of it as an "all or nothing" situation. Most of your infant's nutrition will still come from breastmilk/formula. Your child might simply spit the solid food out, or seem to lose interest. Just keep at it a little at a time and before you know it, your child will be eating regular foods along with everyone else. Here are some tips to keep in mind as your child transitions to "people" food:

- Wash your child's hands before he eats. Now that he is grabbing at anything and everything, you will want to make sure any germs your baby has accumulated on his hands don't make it into his mouth while he's eating.

- Many of the solids you will give to your child will need to be in extremely small pieces.
- Only introduce one new food at a time. This way, if your child has an allergic reaction to a food he eats, you will know what the cause is.
- Get prepared for extra cleanup. Babies have not yet mastered the motor skills they use during eating, and spills and messes are the norm.
- Some foods you may want to introduce include chicken or turkey, rice, toast, crackers, and puffs or cereals.
- If your child is teething, which usually begins between 3–6 months depending on the child, some foods that may soothe him are peeled, frozen bananas, frozen bagel pieces, or use a teething ring that has been put in the freezer.
- Your child isn't ready for candy or milk products, raw foods, shellfish, or any other potentially hard-to-chew foods or allergens. If you're not sure, ask your doctor.

Lots and lots of rules! Your child is moving from basically a liquid diet to more of a diet of solid foods. Just remember to keep him on a healthy diet. Getting the proper nutrition into his little body will ensure that he grows and develops to his fullest.

The Weaning Process

I guess the first thing I should do to help my dads out there is to define what exactly the term "weaning" refers to.

This most commonly refers to a gradual decrease in the frequency of breastfeeding for your baby (although I have seen it refer to decreasing bottle feedings as well). This gradual decrease continues to the point where your child is receiving all of his nutrition from solid food and no longer from milk. This process can either be initiated by the baby, who will no longer accept the breast/bottle as his primary food source, or by the parents, who decide the time is right. The American Academy of Pediatrics (*www.aap.org*) states that babies should have milk as their primary food source for the first year of their lives. Weaning may take place as early as month ten, but generally happens later.

So, as you now know, either parents or the child himself can begin the weaning process. You should be ready to offer your BRP support during this time, as she may feel that she's losing a special time that she cherishes between herself and your child. Lots of hugs and assurances are a good place to start!

It's a Fact, Baby!

True or False: Your baby can live off of breastmilk or formula alone.

True. Babies can get the nutrition they need from these sources. Sometimes as early as four months and sometimes as late as 8–10 months is when select solids may be introduced. Please consult your doctor first. This is based on your child's development, ability to sit up and hold his head up strong, and ability to control his mouth and tongue to hold in solid food and swallow, as opposed to his tongue reflexively pushing the food back out.

Sleeping (Months 4–7)

As we have discussed a few times throughout the book, each baby is on a slightly different development schedule. So if we generalize about the milestones attached to a certain month, you may be saying, "Not my baby." But the information is usually tied to a development process that, at one time or another, your child will go through. With that disclaimer out of the way, let's take some time to discuss your child's sleeping habits.

Around the four-month time frame, many parents report that their child regresses in his sleep habits. If he was sleeping substantially through the night (lucky you), often he will begin to wake again, reminding you of a more exhausting and sleep-deprived time of your life a few months ago. Research of various sources seems to indicate that it may be something as simple as children being used to frequent night feedings and their bodies adjusting to a new eating schedule, or looking for some company, or maybe because they are teething and in some discomfort. There are also more complex reasons that may be in play concerning different levels of sleep and how that is changing for your child. One article based on the book *The Wonder Weeks* by Hetty van de Rijt, PhD and Frans Plooij, PhD hypothesizes that babies experience this kind of sleep regression when they are working on a new skill or growth milestone. Regardless, it is important to know that your child will sleep most peacefully in the first part of the night, and tend to cry/sing/rustle/roll after about eight hours of sleep. However, unless you and your BRP are going to bed around 7 P.M. with your baby, it's likely that you'll still be feeling pretty tired during this stage of sleep regression.

Babies do enjoy a good routine so one of the best ways to minimize your child's restless habits is to *stick to a regular sleep schedule*. Keep the naptime's length similar from day to day, and put him to bed for the night at a consistent time. Also, a *bedtime routine* will help your child wind down for the night. Whether you give him a bath, read him a story, or some of both, keep a routine before putting your child to bed.

When your child wakes up during the night, and invariably he will, you and Mom can decide if you are going to run to your child or simply let him cry it out. Our pediatrician, whom I love, told us to set a time limit if we couldn't agree on one method or the other. So after ten minutes, if she was still crying, one of us would go in and rock-and-walk until sleep came. Our pediatrician reasoned that if our bundle of joy had not stopped after ten minutes, by that time she had cried herself fully awake and would likely need help getting back to sleep. Some parents are quite firm and refuse to enter their child's room between certain hours to allow him to learn to put himself back to sleep faster. It's really up to you how to play it. When—not if—your child hits a rough patch, it will affect your and Mom's sleep schedules as well. Be creative on ways to combat exhaustion, such as taking turns rocking the baby back to sleep and giving each other time to nap when possible. Anything you can do to keep each other as rested as possible will help.

Chapter 5

Crib Notes

- Your child's physical and cognitive development will continue as he starts to learn new things. You will see (and hear) these skills in action!
- As your child approaches six months of age, he may begin teething. This is a precursor to his baby teeth showing up.
- Six or seven months in, your child will gain some mobility on his own. It will be time to see if you did a good job babyproofing your home.
- It may be time to introduce solids into your child's diet. Most of his nutrition will still come from breastmilk/ formula as solids are slowly added.
- Progress is always the order of the day, except when it comes to your child's sleeping habits. Many infants actually regress and awaken more often during the night at this age.

CHAPTER 6

Taking Care of Mom

Taking care of your BRP is now a very important part of your life. Men tend to like their castle to be orderly and things to run smoothly, and that's not always the case when you have a new baby in the mix. Well, there is an axiom that holds true: when Momma's happy, everyone is happy. Buying Mom an iPad (which will act like a grownup pacifier) may tide her over for a few weeks, but what are you going to do when the bloom is off that rose? You need to take care of your family and tackle any problems that seem to be going on at home; you two are a team after all. In this chapter, we'll discuss a few strategies that will help keep the glass half full in your home long after the thrill of playing "Angry Birds Space" has worn off.

Know Your Role

What is the role of the modern day "Dad"? Now, I don't expect you to answer, as you just recently added "Dad" to your life resume. But I am going to ask you to come along with me and give it some thought.

. . .

What did you come up with? Nothing? Okay, because this is a conversation, I will help get you started. Ultimately, your role will be to be whatever your family needs. Sound overwhelming? Well, hopefully you and Mom have split up the household and childrearing roles/duties amongst yourselves. You should have her back, and she should have yours. As we have discussed, the most important indicator of a child growing up in good condition is when his parents are together. Your kids need you.

If evolution really works, how come mothers only have two hands?
—Milton Berle

So, as your family grows, what exactly you need to do will start to become clear. Someone—or two someones—has to work and earn money. Chores need to be done. Your child's needs have to be taken care of.

But know that you do have your work cut out for you. You will be fighting the past reality of less involved dads-as-parents, and the continuing perception that only a minority of dads are pulling their weight. When I brought up this topic as a kind of mad science experiment, it brought instant feedback from many women that their husbands aren't doing their 50 percent, and perusing a few popular Motherhood blogs only showed this sense of inequality again. So, by taking on the role of being an active parent and partner to your BRP, you will be, in essence, attempting to redefine how fathers are thought of today. So don't fall into the trap of thinking to yourself that just going to work is "enough." Even if you are allowed to do this by your forgiving BRP, you are missing out. By doing your part with the household, and as a parent, you will only develop a stronger family bond with both the mother of your child and your child as well. When you stop to think about it, it is quite a good payoff for doing your part! You are a pioneer on par with the likes of Christopher Columbus and Lewis and Clark. Once you have decided to step up and take on this role of the "new" breed of father, you now know what must be done. You have figured out your role.

Just keep in mind that, when there's a baby in the house, the two parents need to take care of their child, and of each other. Like the old saying goes . . .

Moms and Dads: Teamwork Makes Winners

The sports analogy really does work here. You and Mom are in charge of the household, and have certain responsibilities. If you two are not handling your responsibilities, then the house becomes very disorganized and it makes it very difficult for the kids. It is like when there is a lack of leadership on your team, it makes it very hard to win. You and your BRP, whatever your relationship is like today, tomorrow, or next week, are teammates in this parenting task. So be good teammates to each other. But what makes a good teammate?

- **Be on the same page:** You both have to get together and come up with a strategy. Who's taking Junior to daycare this week? Did you buy more diapers? Whose turn is it to go out partying with your friends this weekend? (Trick question: it's time for you guys to tone it down!) Your ability to plan together to take care of the business at hand will be a huge part of your lives running smoothly. Best-case scenario is to take some time Sunday night to plan out the week. Often plans will be made (and change) on the fly.

- **Pick up the slack:** When one or the other of you turns up sick, or has to put in extra time at the workplace, will the other be there to take on extra responsibility? As you will most likely see, things are not always going to be "fair" between Mom and Dad on any given day. You may have to do more than your share to keep your family unit running smoothly. Be prepared to do so, and best case, do the same again tomorrow.

- **Don't keep score:** This is probably the biggest one from my experience as well as anecdotal evidence. There will be plenty of times when "undesirable activity X" will arise, usually involving changing your child's diaper when you are at a party/just sat down for dinner/etc. My advice: step up. "But I did it last time" will eventually lead to two tired, grumpy parents dredging up "that one time" when the other was a little lazy in his or her duties. It's a dead-end street. Just imagine taking the lead and grabbing that child every time the diaper looks extra saggy. What's the worst that could happen?

- **Help out:** Say you, prebaby, call your significant other about 3 P.M. Friday afternoon and inform her there is a slight modification in the plan, as in, you are going out with the guys. She can get mad, or rustle up a few friends of her own. But it changes when you say, Friday at 3 P.M., "I am leaving you at home with our magnificent pooping creation while I go goof off." It doesn't matter if you are going to the public library or the pub crawl. You're not helping. You should know how your actions or lack of action may impact your BRP, and vice versa. I called you out first because men have a spotty track record on this subject historically.

- **Don't ambush:** Don't set your BRP up to be the bad guy or buzzkill. If a group of your friends is going somewhere, perhaps to a certain town in the state of Nevada, don't call her to ask if it is okay with her if you go ahead and book your flight while your friends chant your name in the background. You are setting her up and manipulating her, which isn't really playing nice with others. As we discussed, this isn't just about her having to find a good movie to go to while you are out deciding whether or not you should stand on "16" with the dealer showing a "7." Whoever is taking care of your child could be in for long, sleepless nights and, with no help, getting up and doing it all over again solo.

- **Watch your internal monologue:** Monitor your inner conversation with yourself. If you find yourself having a lot of negative stream of consciousness concerning your BRP, there is a problem. Just be careful; often times in a long-term relationship when you think it's your partner's fault, it is almost always at least partially yours. Why is this important to parents? Because both of you are giving of yourselves to support your child. From time to time, both of you will feel overwhelmed and wonder why nobody is helping you more. You will blame each other. So monitor what's going through your head, and give each other the benefit of the doubt whenever you're strong enough to do so.

These are some of the methods and thoughts to keep in mind. You can take these concepts and apply them to situations you will confront in everyday life. Play fair, try to put yourself in your BRP's shoes, and redefine what it means to be a father today. That is all the world will ask of you. You've become the king of your own castle, and heavy indeed is the head that wears the crown. As the king, sometimes the best way to win, a.k.a. have peace and harmony in your castle, is to lose. Namely, lose an argument or agree to compromise to keep everyone together, which will help you draw strength and satisfaction from the fact that your family is happy. Now isn't that more important than the 3rd quarter of the Independence Bowl or whether or not you have taken out the trash 843 straight times? Do whatever the unwanted chore of the moment may be, once more, and get on with things. When you do enough of these good deeds on a consistent basis, you may just earn a few brownie points from Mom . . .

It's a Fact, Baby!

Do you know when Mother's Day began in the United States?

1914. Yes, we have been celebrating mothers for a long time in our country. By the way, you have a new holiday to be responsible for. On the gift-giving spectrum, I rate it behind Christmas and her birthday, but bigger than Valentine's Day. Do you know when it is? You better mark your calendar. Mother's Day is the second Sunday in May.

Brownie Points with Mom

The two of you are venturing into unknown waters in your relationship. If you are a chronic overachiever, perhaps the two of you attended some sort of workshop or class—like a birthing class, childcare class, CPR course, etc.—in preparation for the arrival of your child. But complex relationships are almost always different in practice than they are in theory. Otherwise "diet and exercise" would be the fad diet we would all follow. So when the changes happen that come with having a child take over your lives, don't let them overwhelm you. Adapt and evolve into a strong father and supportive partner. Your BRP, whether she stays home or goes back to work, needs your support.

One of the best ways to support your BRP is to spoil her, earn brownie points with her, etc. After all, working on your relationship with Mom is also what's best for your child. Weird how that works, isn't it? Basically what all of these various phrases about working on your relationship and being supportive boil down to is you making the extra effort. Make the extra effort to understand her. Try to find ways to make her day just a little easier. Your relationship has changed since your child arrived. You don't have as much time alone together, just the two of you, and between your various responsibilities and the sleep deprivation, there will come some challenges. But I have always found it to be effective to, instead of telling her you're committed to the family, *show* her instead. It can be easy to feel those good intentions as you leave for work, only to come home and succumb to the couch or television while she picks up your slack. At this point you may be saying to yourself, "Why doesn't she 'step up' and rub my feet after a long day?" Well, the first reason is your feet probably smell. The second thing is, as we've discussed, it truly doesn't matter what the score is in your daily life together.

Take it upon yourself to be the initiator, the one who is always there to hold things together. You may be surprised when it comes back to you in spades. So spoil Mom. Treat her like your queen. What does she truly enjoy? It could be as simple as a family picnic, a drive on a scenic road, or going for a long walk together with Junior in the stroller. My point is, it does not have to be expensive!

It's a Fact, Baby!

True or False: Although getting lots of sleep is nice, adults do not need more than five hours per night.

False. Research shows that only 3 percent of adults have the genetic makeup to thrive on less than the rec-ommended 7.5 hours (or more) of nightly sleep. To the dads out there, to answer your question, no, that gene is not called "being tough."

Mars, Meet Venus: Understand Your Differences

As a new dad, it's important for you to realize, as I hope we can all agree, that moms and dads are fundamentally dif-ferent. Dads, in my experience, often are satisfied to make the best of a bad situation, and not be overly distraught if the result of the day is "good enough." But your BRP, dif-ferences in anatomy aside, is a different animal. And, well, relationships are a two-way street. You know her, and she knows you, but you are both changing, becoming different versions of yourselves. The hope here is that you are the first to step forward and say that you accept her for who she's becoming. She is the one you choose. You hope she does the same in return for you.

One of the things that makes any long-term relationship difficult is the differences between people, and while they can help spark an interest, they can also be a source of friction in your relationship. Men and women have some pretty major differences, and while differences of opinion or taste in music are often easy to deal with and are often interesting, differences in parenting philosophy can be very difficult to overcome. Say you believe in spanking your children, and Mom does not. Mom thinks Junior should never be watched by anyone other than family, and you think the local teenager could cover you guys for a few hours. Different parental philosophies and attitudes can lead to, um, spirited discussions (a.k.a. fights) between parents. These differences can enrich your child in the long-term, but cause disagreements as well. Enjoy!

In addition to philosophical parenting differences, there is something about moms that I will probably never fully understand: the inane pressure they put on themselves to be perfect. Moms want the greeting-card life for themselves and their families. A perfect example to me are the Christmas cards that we receive and send out every year. First, many men could take or leave this practice altogether. If we were left in charge of the project, we might come up short in the areas of "theme" and "outfit coordination." But, since your BRP probably takes charge of this part of the holidays, the cards we send out show all smiles, perfect color coordination, and often portray a Rockwellian scene. Like, here we are, stain-free and in our Christmas colors, chopping down last year's Christmas tree in a snow-covered forest, holding mugs of steaming cocoa while various wildlife looks on. Peace on Earth and goodwill toward men. But back in the real world, the kids were complaining the whole time, the deer and birds were photoshopped, and Dad switched his cocoa for a thermos full of Scotch. But if your significant other feels this pressure to be perfect, things like the Christmas card will be important to her. Now that's great information and insight, but how does that help you as a parent? Just remember that, when you are doing your 1,000th take of the Christmas card photo, it really may be coming from a place in your BRP where she feels pressure to give the perfect life to her family. I know when I realized this, it made it easier to work with her instead of moaning, groaning, and generally making things more difficult. The best guideline, for this and many other scenarios you may find yourself in, is "if it is important to her, then it's important to me." Keep that always in your mind, and you will have taken a huge step to having a happy BRP, and a happy household.

Her Health

New moms are under a lot of pressure. If your BRP has decided to breastfeed, it will be important for her to get regular rest, and to maintain a healthy diet. After all, what she eats, the baby eats. Similar to during the pregnancy, she will need to limit alcohol (most say one to two drinks per week max). The good news is she can have some caffeine at least (most moms that is, check with your doctor). If your child has colic, there are many foods that worsen the condition and should be avoided, such as alcohol, spicy foods, and some vegetables. Also, if your BRP is breastfeeding, she will need to drink lots of water to stay hydrated. Put all these rules and regulations together and that's a lot of pressure for anyone! In turn, it is your responsibility, Dad, to support her by living the same way.

Boot Camp

In addition to diet and staying mentally positive, your BRP will have physical issues she will be recovering from postbirth. The general rule after a natural birth is to wait six weeks before she begins an exercise program, and longer if she delivered via C-section. Either way, she needs to get clearance from her doctor. But having a doctor-approved exercise routine is very important, as this will help her body strengthen and recover from giving birth, and may ward off (or lessen) common postpregnancy issues such as fatigue, muscle and back ache, and weight gain.

Good Vibrations

In addition to supporting your BRP's efforts to stay healthy for your baby, you also need to try to find ways to keep each other mentally positive. After all, your BRP may be feeling a little overwhelmed at this time. If you are the breadwinner, then it is up to her alone to care for your child while you're at work. If both of you work, then she may feel the pressure of missing any of your child's accomplishments and she may be jealous of women who stay home with their children. These are traps that many women fall into. They often feel pressure, as if they will be negatively judged if not everything is perfect and they're having trouble "having it all." It's your job to support her and make sure that you are doing your part (or even a little extra when it is called for) and that both of you are watching out for each other.

But sometimes, us men simply cannot quite "get it." I do not say this with sarcasm or bitterness. I truly speak from experience. So how can we help even if we don't understand how our BRPs are feeling during this time? Here are some tried and true methods:

- **Mom's morning out:** Get her to join one of these groups of new mothers in your area. They get together with other mothers and give each other that extra support they need. It's like you and your weekly poker games, without the cigars and alcohol.
- **Give her regular breaks:** Make sure you give her guilt-free time away from the baby. She will need it. Let her go to the gym, take a nap, whatever she needs to recharge. Don't worry. Your turn will come.
- **Couples time:** Find a set of grandparents or a trusted babysitter to come over so you two can spend some time together. I don't care if you take a picnic basket and candles into the backyard. You will both need this time to reintroduce yourselves to each other.
- **Watch the blues:** You both need to agree to watch out for one another's mental state, and give each other permission to say, "Hey, are you okay?" It is estimated that anywhere from 10–25 percent of moms experience postpartum depression, and most cases are unreported. This can take hold anywhere from at the hospital to several months after. It makes it harder for anyone to tell the difference when Mom and Dad are perpetually exhausted anyway. So watch each other's back, and if there is any doubt, go see a doctor for goodness' sake. Getting help early is so much better than trying to go it alone.

Because we're talking about "her health" here, we really dug in to find tips and actions you can take to keep Mom healthy both mentally and physically. Even if she is tackling these things on her own without much prodding from you, it would behoove you to quit horsing around and join her in her efforts. In addition to exercising with her when possible, doing things like helping plan a healthy menu together for the week will help keep both of you in sync and be one more activity you do together. What else can you do? Heck, throw on the "Kiss the Cook" apron and prepare dinner a couple nights a week. If she is required to reduce or eliminate certain items from her diet, say, like alcohol or caffeine, then as a sign of solidarity give those things up also. If you want to, the opportunities to love and support your BRP are almost limitless.

Having a baby changes the way you view your in-laws. I love it when they come to visit now. They can hold the baby and I can go out.
—Matthew Broderick

Sex

Now since we're talking about your BRP's health, it seems like a good spot to talk about sex. There are all kinds of factors that can bring changes to your sex life in your brave new postbaby world. The main thing is that Mom's body has been through a lot. Can we all agree that we conceptually understand how giving birth can be extremely hard on a woman's body without going into a detailed medical discussion? Please? Okay good. Let's continue . . . So after the baby is born, most doctors recommend that you wait at least four weeks until sex. If there were any stitches required (and shouldn't we just leave it at that?), then it will most likely trend out to six weeks, and then only if her doctor gives her the green light.

It's a Fact, Baby!

Respect your doctor's advice on the postbirth time frame to begin having sex again. Do you know the record for the shortest recorded time between births?

Guinness Book of Records states that in 1999–2000, a New Zealand woman gave birth to children a mere 208 days apart. I wonder if they had the fortitude to have another baby shower?

Okay. So you have steeled yourself for four or possibly six weeks and a doctor's note before "the pants party" gets started. But more caution may be required. First of all, you have to put yourself in your BRP's shoes. Not to try to dissuade you from getting back on the horse, but here are some of the obstacles you are facing when the two of you are returning to the boudoir for the first time after the baby has arrived:

- **Pain:** Her first thought will probably be concerning pain, and if she will have any during sex. This is especially true if she had any perineal tearing or an episiotomy. Simply because the doctor gives the two of you the green light does not mean that it is automatic.

- **Low Libido:** Why does "libido" sound like a word being spoken by a man wearing polyester bell bottom pants, platform shoes, and a peace symbol necklace. Anyway, there is evidence that new mothers will often experience a lower sex drive. This will be passed on to you, as when one of the participants in the two-person activity isn't as interested, there is a greater chance you will see a reduced frequency in sexual relations.

- **Changes:** Let's recap, shall we? Mom has just given birth, and whether it was traditional or via C-section, her body went through a lot. She may be breastfeeding or pumping breastmilk, which requires more of her time and energy. On top of this, your child is still settling into his schedule. Your BRP is also trying to live up to the pressure of being the perfect mother from day one. You can and will get back to the physical aspect of your relationship, but with so much going on in your lives, it may take a little while.

So have I dampened your enthusiasm? Did you think this section of the book would be more Kama Sutra rather than a cold splash of water? There are tons of physical and emotional demands that are required of new parents, and you will have to adjust accordingly—and be respectful of your BRP along the way.

Chapter 6

Crib Notes

- The role of the modern dad is still changing and evolving. Communicate with your BRP to find each of your roles.
- If you are committed to making your family work, don't keep score with one another. If you take the first step and take on extra responsibility, it will come back to you in spades.
- Moms are under pressure, if from nobody else, then from themselves. They feel the need to be perfect. Perfect house, perfect at work, and being an all-world mother. Give her the support she needs.
- Mom may need the additional support from a mother's group in your area. Also make sure to set aside some time for the two of you to be alone.
- The "baby blues" are just a nice name for postpartum depression. Both you and your child's mother need to look out for one another and make sure you are just tired or having a bad day, and not becoming depressed. If either of you are unsure about what you are feeling, seek some help or support from a professional.

CHAPTER 7

Your Health

Throughout the book, we've spent lots and lots of time discussing how you'll be caring for your new baby—they are kinda helpless after all—and in the last chapter, we took a look at Mom's health, both physical and mental. It is quite important to help and support your BRP, as she is often the one placing hugely unrealistic expectations on herself to be a perfect mom and solve world hunger while she is at it. But it seems as though there is somebody else you should spend some time focusing on as well . . .

You!

We need to take a look at the things you should be doing to take care of yourself. The more you feel nervous, anxious, stressed out, or just plain terrified about your new life, the more this chapter could be a step in the right direction to help you out. You can cut it out and tape it above your mirror, or tattoo the entire section onto your body to serve as a reminder. Just make sure you get the title and author in large font. I could use the publicity.

Physical

So it is good for you to take stock of yourself physically. What's the score? By that I mean many things, but to start, are there any drastic changes occurring? You are probably getting less sleep, and you have less time for yourself. Are you still exercising? A quick trip around suburbia will show that weight gain is the devil most parents are dealing with. If you start gaining or losing weight (a change of roughly 5–10 percent increase should be a warning sign) due to your new life, then it is time to reassess your strategy. Look, we're not talking about you starting a new hardcore health regimen. Walking or working out three to four times a week for at least 30 minutes is a good place to start, and you and your BRP can even work together to help each other get regular exercise. Strangely enough, not only will a light amount of exercise help you stay in shape and manage your weight; it will relieve mental stress. As always, consult with your doctor, attorney, and spiritual guru before starting any exercise program. Here are a few ideas to get you started:

- **Walk:** It seems overly simple and rudimentary, just walking. One foot in front of the other, over and over again. But getting outside, getting the blood pumping, and getting some natural sunlight will do wonders for you hardcore office dwellers out there.
- **Home Gym:** Put Junior in an age-appropriate support seat with toys and see how far you can go on that stationary bike (not very). Play fun, upbeat music and interact with your child while you get in a good sweat. Babies love music!

- **Extreme Stroller Running:** Invest in a slightly used jogging stroller (trust me when I tell you that these things can be pretty expensive) and take your child out for a few laps around the park or neighborhood. It is quite simple: all you need to do is run! Whether you do this together with Mom, or just let her catch up on some much-needed sleep, then you just hit the "double word" bonus. Keno!

These are some simple yet effective ideas for you to get back into some sort of exercise program in your new lives together. The research proves that you need to exercise at least 3–4 times per week to stay reasonably healthy. In addition to your physical health, we need to explore other areas as well . . .

It's a Fact, Baby!

True or False: Adults need at least 40 minutes per week of moderate exercise (running/jogging) to maintain a healthy lifestyle.

False. Per the CDC, adults need at least 75 minutes of running/jogging weekly, plus two days a week of muscle-strengthening exercises for all muscle groups.

Mental

How is your mental fitness? Never heard of it? Well, when I speak about mental health, I am talking about your ability to deal with the highs and invariable lows that life brings you; your emotional well-being, if you will. In a world far, far away from this one, if you needed to give yourself a little boost and take some "me" time, it was really no problem.

But like a toddler giving up his pacifier, new parents often struggle when they realize that between all of their responsibilities, there is very little time left for them to care for themselves. As this realization sinks in, reactions can vary from frustration to anger. This is no temporary situation: you will be a parent forever. So if you find yourself frustrated very often during the day, tend to lose your temper, and generally feel like you are not yourself (where did you go?), then there are some steps you can take to improve your outlook.

- **Let your mind wander:** Let your mind drift, float, and exist in the moment. Some call this daydreaming, others meditation. But taking a break from the stresses you face is a way to clear your mind and approach obstacles with a fresh outlook. Prayer, meditation, or jamming out to your favorite oldies (in the car if you must) are some quick ways to break out of a negative mental state and re-energize yourself to face the day.
- **Focus:** Your "to-do" list has grown out of control. It is full of work and home items that seem insurmountable. As you run through the list mentally, your brain shoots in different directions about the things you must accomplish at work; how you need to get your car into the shop for maintenance; and, oh yeah, it is your week to do the grocery shopping. So break out a paper and pen and make a list of everything you have to do. Then rank them in order of what needs to be done first. Then break that down into what you can do *today*. This is taking control of things and improving your focus. It has been proven that multitasking does not help, so stick to doing just one thing at a time. And if one of those other tasks rears its ugly

head, you will know where it falls on your list and won't feel further stress.

- **Exercise:** By the time you finish this chapter, you will be convinced I am going to try to sell you "The Pfeiffer Exerciser" total fitness gym. Maybe I should . . . But while that's in development, find an exercise activity that you look forward to. It should match your personality. Seeking solitude? Running may be a good fit. Feeling lonely? A fitness club or gym may be the answer. Yes, physical and mental health are tied together, so "Just do it." Studies show that cardiovascular exercise like running or bike riding, Zumba, etc., can release chemicals in the brain that improve and stabilize your moods. Amazing thing, the human body.

- **Get a hobby:** Find some time for yourself by finding a hobby to pour your energy into. Build a model plane, figure out how to put one of those ships into a bottle, or write that book you have been meaning to write (just not a pregnancy and parenting book—there's already too much competition).

- **Set goals and rewards:** Set up your goals for the day, week, and month. They can be as specific or general as you want, but they should be more specific than "Monday: exist." Set up rewards for yourself that fit. No, you don't get a new car if you attend work five days in a row, or if you remember to pick up diapers from the store on the way home from work. Try to pick goals that fit the criteria of "challenging yet attainable." But a nice steak or a special family activity would be nice. If you pick something too large, then you have to feel guilty about your reward, which sucks and defeats the purpose of the reward in the first place.

- **Go forth and do good works:** Volunteering can be a way to recharge yourself mentally. Now, you don't have to fly to Darfur and try to make a difference. There are likely undermanned community centers and soup kitchens aplenty in your area. Volunteer to help out at an event that you are interested in, like a local 10K that is a fundraiser for a cause you believe in. It may spur you on to your own goals.

- **Spend a minute getting to know *you*:** Now, you may give some of these activities a try only to find that they don't really work for you. You daydreamed about playing the guitar, and after a month of lessons, you find out you have no desire to become a local coffee shop legend. That's no problem. It's called personal growth. If you have ruled something out, then try to find something else that renews and recharges you. Some people run marathons. Others build sandcastles. Some may paint or keep a journal. Once you find that magical something that fits in your life and makes you feel like you are flying—and like yourself again—you will know it.

As a parent, it's in your nature to want to pour everything you have into your children. But in reality, that isn't the way to do it. You and your BRP need to make time to take care of each other and yourselves to stay happy and healthy. In the end, it will actually make you a better parent because you will be better able to deal with your suddenly hectic lifestyle. It will also help you avoid many health concerns ranging from the common cold to depression. So make time to take care of yourselves, and if your BRP isn't doing it, go the extra mile to make sure she has the time.

It's a Fact, Baby!

True or False: New dads can suffer postpartum depression.

True. It is shown that just over 10 percent of dads get something akin to postpartum depression before their child's first birthday. It is quite possibly higher, as men aren't known to always report it when it occurs. Who says we don't understand what women are going through?

Vasectomy: To Snip, or Not to Snip

Okay men, we have reached that sensitive area that makes us all cringe. For the next few minutes, I am going to be figuratively in your pants. Like any stressed out new dad, you are going to be wondering if you are going to want any more children. If the answer to that question is a definite "YES!" then good for you, and move on to the next section. If the answer is, "Love the one(s) I got, but this is it, man," then at some point you will most likely begin to wonder, "Should I get a vasectomy?" Right away a feeling of fear will penetrate your brain. Visions of grapefruits or other large, circular fruits may begin to enter your mind. You have heard the horror stories, and imagined them as well. Well, let's get the truth out there.

It's a Fact, Baby!

What percentage of men 35 or over get a vasectomy?

In 2010, records indicate around 17 percent of men over the age of 35 have had a vasectomy.

Pros and Cons?

I do not know your reason for considering this procedure, but overwhelmingly the men going for it are married. Specifically, a vasectomy is a safe and very effective procedure used to sterilize men. The doctor of your choosing applies local anesthetic and cuts the vas deferens tubes that transport sperm into the launch area. Once the vas deferens is cut, the sperm does not get transported into the body for release. Less specifically, it's like the villain on the TV show cuts the brake lines, and the sperm car doesn't work anymore. After the procedure, you can still have sex (hooray!) and really will not notice any difference. The benefits are that you will not have to use a condom to prevent pregnancy (the chance of pregnancy is reduced to one in 1,000), and your partner will not have to deal with any of the various methods of birth control available, or undergo surgery herself to be sterilized. As one woman put it, "The surgery options are easier on men than the options for women." You will have to ask yourself some tough questions about whether you would *ever*, under any circumstances (divorce, death of spouse, etc.), want to have children again. Vasectomies are potentially reversible, but there is no guarantee that the reversal will work. So when I say you need to be sure, I mean it.

What Does It Involve?

What about the procedure itself? It usually only requires about an hour, and the doctor only uses a local anesthetic. You are, for better or for worse, awake the whole time. For many of you, your insurance coverage will even pay for this procedure. As the doctor I spoke with said, "You can have the procedure Friday afternoon, rest during the weekend, and be back to work on Monday." He also stressed that you would want to think twice before doing any extremely stressful exercise or heavy lifting for a week or two. Why do you need to wait? It is mostly because it will feel like you are being repeatedly punched in the groin if you exercise too soon. I think the legal team would like it if I wrapped this section up with a disclaimer that vasectomies do not prevent sexually transmitted diseases. Are we in good shape? Okay, let's move on.

Work/Life Balance: What's That?

Wait, what is work/life balance? In its most basic form, it is balancing your duties to your family and yourself with your commitment to your career. This became more important recently as more and more employers are asking employees to work nontraditional schedules and fifty-hour work weeks are becoming the norm instead of the exception. You simply cannot keep this type of work schedule and have much quality time left over to spend with your family. If your schedule becomes work, reheated dinner, and fifteen minutes with your child, you have no balance. And without balance, all that is left is "work." Some people choose this for themselves, and I am in no position to judge. But for many of us, we do not wish to miss all the birthdays, recitals, and school plays that you can only see once.

Now without a healthy work/life balance, I would have no idea who Mr. Miyagi is (or was, RIP Pat Morita). But just taking some time to see a few movies, is that work/life balance? Not exactly. And, if you decide to blow out of the office at 4 P.M. to go have drinks, that's not really work/life balance either. Basically, you need to have meaningful effort and accomplishment in the important areas of life, which include your work, family, friends, and yourself. Achievement and recognition at work, deep and loving bonds with family and friends, and living the life you want to live are all so important to keep in mind as you strive to progress on each of these fronts on a daily basis.

Can work alone make you the best version of yourself? Is it your work life that defines who you are and what your value is to the world? One way to see if your are experiencing work/life balance is to write down all of the labels that you believe apply to yourself. Employee, father, husband, brother, and whatever else you throw in there. Now, record the hours during the next week or two that you spend under each heading. It will give you an idea of whether you need to redefine yourself, and what kind of balance you are achieving, if that's your goal. If your goal is to go as far up the company ladder as fast as you can, you will see that represented here as well. But that is why it is called "work/life balance." Because it will be a precarious balancing act to achieve everything that you want in all areas of your life. By monitoring where you are spending your time and energy, you can gain perspective on whether you are being the man you want to be.

Better learn balance. Balance is key.

Balance good, karate good. Everything good.

Balance bad, better pack up, go home. Understand?

—Mr. Miyagi, The Karate Kid

Chapter 7

Crib Notes

- While you are adjusting your life to take care of your growing family, you need to make sure that you are taking care of yourself as well.
- Consistent physical activity contributes countless benefits to both your physical and mental health.
- You will face many highs and lows in your life. The important thing is how you decide to deal with them.
- Any long-term relationship, including a marriage, requires effort to stay vibrant and healthy.
- Financial and sexual issues are the top two reasons spouses list as the cause of their divorce.
- Find time to unwind and relax your mind. Give yourself permission to think about something besides the pressure and stress of everyday life.
- If you are sure that you do not desire additional children, you may want to consider a vasectomy as a safe and efficient way to prevent future pregnancies.
- Work/life balance is a complex topic. At the root of it is finding satisfaction and enjoyment out of the most important areas of your life as you define them.

CHAPTER 8

Welcome (Back) to the Outside World

You, your BRP, and your new baby have been in your home, adjusting to each other, getting your schedule together. Early on, you may have been fortunate enough to have substantial help taking care of your child from grandparents or your extended family. In your safety bubble at home, you have control—more or less—over your environment: You can control the noise level, naptimes, and how clean your house is (or isn't!). But eventually, you are going to have to swallow the real world, straight, no chaser. Out there, chaos reigns supreme, you have bills to pay and work to get done, and other parents judge your parenting style. In this chapter, let's take a look at some of the difficulties you will face going forward.

Competitive Parents

Judge-y, competitive parents are one of my least favorite phenomena observed in the suburban jungle today. Say you are at a local park, enjoying a sunny day with your child. A parent comes over to chat, you know, chew the fat about parenting and how cute both of your children are. Instead, it turns into a conversation about how *their* baby accomplished "milestone X" *way* before your child, and how their child is learning Mandarin, and oh by the way, the clothes your child is wearing have been recalled because they are actually known to spontaneously combust, and . . . have a nice day. Yes, it is basically one big guilt trip, guaranteed to make you feel inadequate as a parent. Here is the deal. If they tell you something that you didn't know that's important and can help your child, like the flammable clothes thing, then you need to be the bigger person and learn from it. But also do not feel like a bad parent. There are two things you have to remember about these kind of people: 1) Their actions make it seem like they are bragging about beating you during the first half-mile of a marathon, which doesn't make any sense because there's a long way to go yet. 2) It's like the "fly" on their pants is open: they are showing you how petty they are and their need to make themselves feel superior. Good parenting can take many, many forms. Only you know what is best for your family and your child. Work hard, parent hard, and be secure in the knowledge you are the best man for the position. Of course, if you see another parent do something brilliant, don't be afraid to steal it immediately!

Working with "The Schedule"

"The Schedule" and "The Calendar" will take on all new meaning for you and your BRP once your child enters the mix and the make-believe world of maternity/paternity leave ends (if you were lucky enough to get it in the first place). But when you emerge into the real world, scheduling conflicts will inevitably arise between your family. You and your BRP have activities and hobbies, a social calendar, and jobs. Your child will have a nap schedule, feeding schedule, and, unfortunately, is not old enough to go to work with you. So what you need to focus on here are two things that take some getting used to: coordination and sacrifice.

If you are both working, you will need to consider several issues depending on your situation. If one of you is offered a promotion that will require more hours at the office and greater travel, then the other parent will have to adjust accordingly. I mean, what if you both have to travel for work? There's no such thing as a twenty-four-hour daycare facility. The only moving part here could be if you *both* take big promotions and earn the big bucks, then you could possibly get a nanny, au pair, or pay a grandparent for his or her services. No matter your situation, if you're both working, then you and your BRP will need to split up or outsource all of those duties that are associated with the home. Write them all down, throw them in a hat, and draw. List them all out and take turns picking. Treat it like your fantasy league draft, and then you can make trades with each other.

If only one of you is working and is able to provide for the family, then you are a step ahead of most. The percentage of two-income parents was in about the 58 percent range in 2010. I would hazard a guess that this is financially motivated, and most are not working for the "love of the game." When you fall in this category, the tradeoffs are different. The stay-at-home parent needs to be considerate and mindful of the challenges of the workplace. The house and child and all of the duties contained therein become this person's domain. You should not really expect to drop a crying baby into your partner's arms the minute she enters the home. (PS: no chauvinism is intended here. In 2005, 16 percent of young, school-aged children were primarily cared for by their dads. I suspect that number is rising.) Although the pay is nonexistent, if you're the at-home parent, attack the daily work with the ferocity of a loan shark looking to collect. The one problem you will discover is that your office never closes. You are open for breakfast, lunch, dinner, and even the occasional midnight snack seven days a week—and for sick or crying children, you are open twenty-four hours a day. With this in mind, try to find a night, weekly or monthly, where you can either go out to eat, or if that is not possible, let someone else take over the dinner shift.

If you are the workplace spouse, try not to come home, remove your shoes and socks, and wait for the foot massage to begin. Try to find some household "opportunities" for you to help out. Maybe it is something as simple as taking Junior out to breakfast Saturday morning and giving your significant other some downtime. Don't view household chores as the other parent's sole domain. If you are the breadwinner, wouldn't you appreciate it if the stay-at-home parent found a way to earn a few extra bucks every week? So dive in, put some dishes away, give Junior a bath, and then hang up your cape and recharge for tomorrow.

What I am getting at here is that you need to try and understand what your BRP is going through. You need to have empathy for one another. If you can gain even a partial understanding of what her daily life is, and what her challenges are, it will go a long way toward the two of you staying in touch with each other instead of growing apart. Your relationship will require effort on both your parts to stay healthy.

It's a Fact, Baby!

Is the number of babies born each year trending up or down?

Trending down. The all-time high for recorded births in the United States was in 2007, at just over 4.3 million. That number is down about 7 percent in the latest report. Just think, less competition for your child!

Daycare

It used to be that, if one or both of you work and needed to stay late at the office, it was not a problem. Being considerate involved shooting off a text message, or maybe a quick phone call. But you can't just shoot a text message off to your daycare center. As of today, daycare centers are not open twenty-four hours a day (I hesitate to even float this idea). Most have a final pickup time (usually around 6–6:30 P.M.), and charge something in the neighborhood of $20 a minute if you are late, to encourage parents to arrive to pick up their kids by closing time. If, at this reading, you still have a newborn, you may be tempted to skip this section, as you figure it may not apply to you just yet. But lots of couples begin scouting daycare facilities long before their child will attend, and pay good money to secure their child a spot in just the right facility well in advance of when their child will need to attend daycare. So let's discuss some of the criteria you should consider in the selection process.

When the time comes to select a daycare, you may need to brace yourself. As the saying goes, nobody can care for your child like you can, but you want to find a daycare that comes in at a close second. In my experience, that proverb is played out in the real world in daycare facilities everywhere. It is not that the folks in charge are not well meaning or qualified; it is simply an incredibly difficult task to give proper care and attention to seventeen two-year-olds at the same time. Let's start your journey into the antiseptic-scented world of daycare by looking at some of the basic selection criteria you should look for in a facility:

What Kind of Daycare Are You Looking For?

Only you and your BRP can define which criteria you will use to select a care option for your child. Some of the common factors include criteria such as location, cost, and reputation. However, there are other options available than just your local chain of daycares, and we will briefly look at each to give you a head start in making your decision.

- **Childcare Centers:** These are the most common form of childcare. If you find one of the only 7,000 centers with the NAEYC certification (National Association for the Education of Young Children) then you've hit the jackpot! Otherwise, make sure there are stated guidelines and practices in place for the center so all employees are singing the same song and know what to do during arrival, dismissal, and in other instances like when your child gets sick. Does the facility seem welcoming? Is it well lit? In a good area? These and other criteria we will cover shortly can be a guideline on whether your child will be well cared for at the facility.
- **Childcare Homes:** This is an arrangement that has been around for a long time. You know, your friend down the street is a stay-at-home mother, and needs a

few extra bucks. You need a childcare option you can trust, but don't want to use a daycare. Voila! You pay your friend to take care of your child. Sometimes you will find this arrangement where it is just a nice person in the area who cares for a small number of children out of his or her home. Although states require these homes to be accredited, in reality many of them may not be, especially if the number of children being cared for is small. Use all of the same criteria to evaluate these centers as you would a larger provider. If it is a friend, ask many questions up front in an attempt to avoid an awkward conversation later.

- **In-Home Caregivers:** Many find this option to be the best, but it is also usually the most expensive. This set up usually involves a nanny or someone meeting that general description. The dream of one-to-one care for your child in his own environment is what many think is the next best option to having a parent there to care for a child. When you find the right person, the nanny can become almost like a member of the family you cannot live without. Take good care of her, because she is taking care of your child! Do some additional research on this option if you are seriously considering it. You may have to get an EIN (employer identification number); verify your nanny's right to work in the U.S.; and pay federal income taxes, Social Security tax, and Medicare tax for the paid wages.

In addition to the specific criteria for each different child-care option we touched on, there are some general criteria for each option. Let's take a look at them.

It's a Fact, Baby!

What percentage of kids under the age of 5 are in some form of childcare?

A study done by the Census Bureau released in 2010 states that about 63 percent of children under the age of five have a nonparent childcare arrangement weekly.

Accreditation

Your state has a licensing agency that examines these types of facilities to make sure the basics of cleanliness and safety standards are met for the health and well-being of your child. These are by no means all-encompassing examinations, and the state accreditation is not the gold standard. It is more of a starting point when considering the safety and health of your child. I have actually seen small "in-home" daycares run by really nice people. You may find such a place and decide, accredited or not, this is the place for you. It is my feeling that the bar for this state accreditation is not set at an overly high level. Ergo, if the facility you are considering is not certified, it would raise serious questions in my mind as to what is wrong with the facility. Maybe the lead coating on the toys was a hint? Start your search with state-accredited facilities in your area, and then investigate further from there. At the end of the day, visit as many of these different types of daycares as possible in your geography, and rely on your parental instincts (and your wallet) to make the right call.

Mr. Clean

Or Mrs. Clean, as the case may be. When you take the tour, you can wear white gloves and speak in an English accent, touching the various surfaces to see if they smudge your perfectly pressed *guante*. Or you can just take a hard look around the rooms and eating area to make sure they are frequently cleaned and appear reasonably germ-free. It's really up to you. But don't feel awkward about asking questions about the frequency of cleanings, and the cleaning products used. It is a legitimate question, as daycares are notoriously germ-infested and coughs and colds can spread quickly to all of the kids in the facility.

The Peeps

You know, the people. Try to meet as many of the employees as you can, specifically the person or persons who would be directly looking after your child. Not to get too scientific on you, but when you meet them you should ask yourself: Do they give you the heeby jeebies? Do they creep you out? Because if they do, you will quickly tire of leaving your child with them, and it is time to go to the next place. Ask the owner about his or her employee screening process, and if background checks are performed before hiring. It is also worth poking around and asking some questions about the tenure of the staff. If you ask three or four different people how long they have worked there and each answer is in terms of "weeks" or "months," you know you are looking at a high turnover rate among the workers. Nothing is worse when your child's favorite caregiver at your daycare facility decides it is time to move on, and then your child has to get to know the next person all over again. Not to be dramatic, but it can be traumatic for both you and your child when a fantastic caregiver leaves.

The Curriculum

Of course this doesn't apply to your newborn, whose curriculum consists of eating, sleeping, crying, and waste disposal. But, if nothing else, you can probably infer that a well-thought-out and well-organized program for the older kids means the people in charge have their act together. Look for facilities with a weekly special event like music class or tumbling/gymnastics, for example. One of the better facilities we used had a special activities coordinator who brought in a fun and exciting program once per week. It helped liven things up for the kids. You should also find out about how much time the kids get to play outside (when they are old enough), at what temperatures do they stay inside, what do they do for exercise in the colder months, etc. Because your child may be in different rooms or there may be caregiver turnover, you should receive a daily report on your child (how much they slept, ate, etc.) so you can keep track of how your child is doing.

Technology

There are many facilities that have "nanny cams" where you can log on from any computer, sign in, and see what your child is up to at any given moment. It's nice to be able to check in on Junior. In a Machiavellian or Orwellian twist, it also helps keep teachers on their best behavior. I'm not saying all of them need it, but it never hurts for them to wonder if the parents are watching. Make sure the technology works well and is password protected. You don't need any additional worries about the safety of your child.

Do the Dollars Make Sense?

Obviously, there is a price point where the care for your child would be first-class, but you would probably have to live out of your car to afford it. It's unfortunate that you will have to make tradeoffs based on financial considerations when it comes to the care of your child, but it is also reality. So take location, price, and quality and balance them out to find the best choice for you and your child. In addition, ask your employer about Health Savings accounts.

It's a Fact, Baby!

What is the average annual cost of daycare in the U.S.?

The average cost of center-based care in the U.S. is almost $12,000 a year. In cities like Boston, San Francisco, or New York that average can double and plenty more.

These are programs you may not have been aware of as a childless employee. They basically allow you to pay for childcare with pretax dollars. If you work for a small employer who does not offer this, pursue it because it is generally something fairly easy and inexpensive for them to offer. Make sure to get clarification of the policies. It will be important to know if you need to pay the daycare to keep your spot if you take a week to go see grandma. Some centers will only require a partial payment; others will require the full payment for the week. Either way, this is the kind of thing you will want to know so you can plan accordingly.

Daycare Sick Days

If you are in a situation where your baby will go to daycare, go ahead and discuss this with your doctor. They usually have some time-tested advice that will get your plan of action started, which is a good thing because you should be prepared for your child to get sick often the first few months in childcare. They are exposed to a lot of germs that their bodies have not built up a resistance to. In this vein, try to line up a friend or relative for the first few months for "on-call" duty because daycare centers will often not allow sick children to stay. They will also have a policy for when your child can return after being sick (a common one is no fever for at least twenty-four hours). Inquire as to all of these details. It will help you paint a picture in your mind of how things will go when (not if) your child gets sick. If both parents work, you need to have an action plan for this situation, as in who is going to leave and take care of your baby.

Daycare Hours

Look at the hours of operation for any daycare facility you are considering. Are there work situations that could cause you to need to stay at work beyond what the daycare will allow? On the other side of the issue, is your child allowed to attend daycare part time if you can occasionally work from home? These are the types of questions you need to answer to discover if a daycare is right for your child and you.

Ratios

What are the teacher/caregiver ratios per child? Many facilities will only allow three infants per caregiver for example. As your child gets older, the ratios will increase as infants require a lot of care and attention (as you know by now!). Usually the fewer children per caregiver will also equate to a higher price.

So there you go, a newcomer's primer to the wonderful world of daycare. If your child is beginning daycare soon, then brace yourself. I still remember when I dropped off my kids for the first time. I remember in vivid detail, like you would a terrifying event in your life. There is something about taking your child to the daycare, dropping her off, and then turning and getting back into your car without her that causes a major inflammation of parental guilt. There simply is something not quite right about it. But for better or for worse, it is a necessary evil. You may want to jump up and volunteer for day one drop-off duty, especially if your BRP has been conflicted about it. It's no easy thing. Fortunately it does begin to get easier with time, and as you begin to gain a comfort level with the personnel and facility. If there are any problems, do not be afraid to voice your concerns to the director. This is one service where you *have* to feel a high comfort level and trust. If you don't, then do more research and ask for referrals from friends and neighbors in the area. There is hopefully at least one quality daycare around.

Oh the Places You'll Go (If You're Brave Enough)

At some point in time, you will want to take a vacation. When you take your first vacation with your new baby, be ready for a whole new experience. "Why?" you ask? Haven't you learned anything yet? Vacation planning with a young child is totally different than planning a trip "prebaby." There are all kinds of baby-specific equipment and items that must first be remembered and then packed. Let's get you started on your list:

- **I Lay Me Down to Sleep:** Where is your child going to sleep on this trip? Do you have some sort of portable crib? Or did you bring the "pack 'n play" that Junior likes to nap in so much? Whatever you choose, make sure you have a strategy planned out to keep your child safe and comfortable.

- **White Noise:** Does your child use a "noisemaker" of some sort to help block background noise? If he uses it at home, you will want to bring it along. You basically want your child to be as comfortable as possible to help him sleep. Trying to re-create his home environment as closely as possible is one idea.
- **Life Aid:** Does your trip call for lots of walking? Are you packing that huge stroller that takes up half the trunk? Or are you bringing a more compact model? Depending on your child's age and trip duration, you may need to bring high chairs, bath seats, and bouncy play seats for entertainment purposes.
- **China:** Most likely your baby has his own special set of bottles and bottle warmers, etc., depending on his diet and your routine. You will need to bring it all!

Can you see the picture forming? Are you more understanding of those parents in the minivan with the huge external "egg" strapped to the top to allow for more cargo to be transported?

Keep in mind that some people will totally take their baby with them on any trip, and make it work. Other parents are scared to leave their yard. But if you are a brave soul who chooses to venture forth with your infant, here are some additional factors to consider:

- **The Destination:** Hiking the Appalachian Trail? Planning late dinners and a show in the city that never sleeps? Some trips are best left to adults only. Plan your trip to destinations where families with children are welcome.

- **Baby's Schedule:** The activities you plan to do while on your trip will have to take your child's schedule into account. If bedtime is at 8 P.M., you shouldn't make dinner reservations anywhere but at the drive-through for that ultra-chic "late dinner."
- **Baby's Schedule:** Are you having that déjà vu feeling? Well, if you are a brave soul and decide to travel across time zones, you are most likely a gambler. A one-hour time zone difference is doable, two is dicey, and three hours or international travel is a real world chaos theory experiment, because there is no telling how your child will react.
- **Be Prepared:** Wherever you are heading, get yourself prepared. You should hop on the Internet and locate a doctor/urgent care facility close to your destination, as well as a pharmacy or drug store, with contact numbers, etc. Don't forget the emergency first-aid kit you put together like we discussed! You did prepare one, right?
- **You're Trippin':** I still have scars from one particular trip we took where our newborn cried for the last two-plus hours in the car. We kept thinking she would fall asleep. We pulled off and changed her diaper; we fed her; we tried everything. She wasn't having it. Point being, your young child does not care how much the trip costs, or what your plans are. If she wants to throw a fit, she will. And there is nothing you can do about it. So there.

So you can see the basic thrust here is that by taking your child totally out of her environment and routine, you are inviting unpredictable behavior on her part. So bring your nanny, or be prepared to cut short the activities that you have planned on any given day. You are now less worried about how much those "Black Keys" concert tickets cost, and more worried if Disney on Ice is coming to an arena near you. You moved into a whole different part of your life when you became a parent. I hope by now you are realizing it will affect every part of your life, including work, vacations, free time, sleep schedule, you name it. You are in transition, and don't worry if it is giving you fits along the way. It can do that to people. Gradually the time and effort spent with your child will form a deep bond between you, and making your child happy will make you happy. Before you know it, you will find yourself looking forward to those Disney on Ice tickets.

Chapter 8

Crib Notes

- As your tiny baby gets older, you will start heading out more and more into the outside world where many things are out of your control.
- Parents of other children may be quick to point out areas where they feel their child has advanced further than your child. Remember to take their comments in stride. Raising your child is a marathon, not a sprint.
- Working with the schedule your child has established is very important. Changes in your child's feeding or sleeping schedule can bring about unpredictable behavior.
- Whatever your role within the family—worker or caregiver—have empathy for what your BRP is going through. If you two can strive to understand each other's struggles, it will make you a stronger family.
- If your child is going to daycare, it adds a new layer of complexity to both of your schedules. As parents, you may have to make tough sacrifices to make sure someone is always there for your child when she needs a parent, such as when she is sick. But whatever you do,

put in the time and effort needed to select an appropriate daycare facility. Check their accreditation status, talk to the employees, and generally investigate as much as possible. You are placing your child in these people's care.

- All of this change in your life will likely require you to pause and catch your breath. Planning a vacation with your baby will require you to take her limitations into account and keep flexibility in the schedule to account for downtime for your child.

- You can prepare for your trip by researching the locations of care facilities in the area. If a problem arises, you want to be ready.

- Although there is always an adjustment period for new parents, eventually a strong bond will form with your child and you will look forward to activities you can do as a family.

PART 3

Months 8–12

As your baby starts to grow up, he or she will start to have more grownup problems. We are not talking about shaving or learning to drive; we are more in the realm of weaning and taking his first steps. In this Part, we are going to enter the time when your child starts to show real signs of development. We are passing the initial stage where "baby blinked" or "baby's arm moved" is a big deal. Now, your infant is on the road to becoming a little person. Just watch out, he will be sassing you in no time!

CHAPTER 9

Breaking Developments

Just like in the world of Hollywood or fashion, things go in cycles. What was once old, becomes new again. Change in the past months has given way to more change. But this time the milestones become slightly more significant. No longer are you looking for a nuanced way he grasps a toy or how steadily he holds up his head. Your child is now beginning to move quickly around the house under his own power and is forming a vocabulary of very few recognizable words. I mean what's next, shaving?

Baby's First Steps

Your child is growing and developing in so many ways. The first steps are a timeless milestone that you will want to celebrate. Your child will first learn to roll over, and then crawl. Your baby may not be ready for the dance floor, but he is beginning to crawl forward and gain some ability to move. Watch him extra closely if you use an elevated surface when you change his diaper—he might be on the move!

Around nine months of age, your child will develop the muscle control and strength to pull up to a standing position. At that point, he is in the home stretch. He will steadily progress until around age fourteen or fifteen months, when he should be walking with some level of confidence and stability.

Babies don't need a vacation but I still see them at the beach.
I'll go over to them and say, 'What are you doing here, you've never
worked a day in your life!'
—Stephen Wright

Sleeping (Months 8–12)

For this time period, I will unfortunately stick to the same sleep advice that you've seen in various forms throughout the book. By this point, you and your BRP will be experts on what your baby needs as far as sleeping. But be sure to keep a regular bedtime routine, give your child a chance to put himself back to sleep during the night, and work together with your BRP to grab a quick nap when you can! Developments like erupting teeth and the excitement and high level of brain activity as your child learns new functions like walking (or is starting this process) will lead to some restless nights for your baby. Hang in there!

Separation Anxiety

You know when you used to leave your child with a grandparent or babysitter and there wasn't a problem? You used to think what a wonderful, well-adjusted baby you had. Well, now Junior will realize you are leaving and will cry in protest. This is a natural reaction as baby begins to become more aware of his environment, but it doesn't help ease your (and Mom's) guilt any more.

At this point your child may become especially attached to a blanket or particular stuffed animal. This is a sign he is trying to overcome the dreaded "separation anxiety" when you leave him alone, even at bedtime. This is healthy, as long as he doesn't bring a tattered lovey across the stage at high school graduation. The best way to deal with this situation is to keep your goodbyes short and sweet. Avoid that old parenting trick of sneaking away when he's not looking; many doctors have written that it hurts the child's feelings even more! Separation anxiety often peaks in children between 10–18 months of age, which can seem like a lifetime if they are going to daycare on a regular basis.

Dealing with Temper Tantrums

It's easy to forget your little angel is just a miniature person at this point. He gets tired, frustrated, and irritable just like you do. When he feels frustrated, though, he can't rely on snarky comments or long-winded vents to get it off his chest. So he does what he can at this point in his life: he cries. And boy does he! Do your best to keep your child well rested, fed, and hydrated to prevent these tantrums. That, and if you know from experience that your child throws a tantrum when you take new toys back from him, don't pop into the local toy store just for fun. It is simply inviting trouble.

Playtime

Your child will grow at his own pace in his comfort level playing and interacting with others during this time. Babies under the age of one will generally play more in the same area as each other than any real interaction together. You and your BRP will be his primary playmates until he learns those social skills. So sing with him, dance with him (you lead), and take him on fun outings to age-appropriate destinations such as the zoo or local children's museum. This will help stimulate his little mind. Your baby will also like to play this new game: he throws/drops a toy, food, or other object and watches you fetch. Good times! Keep breakables away; try to only let him get his hands on items you are okay with him playing with.

Little People Exploring a Big World

There are other important changes happening as well. Some will seem so natural that you will hardly notice. Your child has reached the stage where his curiosity outweighs his ability and experience. He wants to explore the world around him, but he is just getting the strength and coordination needed to become mobile. You can be his guide to help him safely explore, learning about the world around him and how to interact with it. Here are some of the highlights:

- **Getting crabby:** We are not talking about your child's mood; he will begin utilizing the pincher grip to pick up things. Just don't let him get anything that might be a choking hazard. Everything he gets his hands on pretty much goes right into his mouth.

- **Just say no!:** Your child will begin to recognize this word, and soon after start doing whatever he wants to anyway (just kidding . . . no really).
- **Take a stand:** Your child will be learning to pull up on the crib, couch, or anything else he can reach. Practice with him to develop strength, and teach him how to sit down from a standing position. Babies like to just "fall" backwards at first.
- **Walkie-talkie:** During this time, babies will really begin to babble with many interesting sounds. They may even hit upon "mama" or "dada." As every parent does, a positive reaction is like telling them, "Hey, you got it right!" It will encourage them to keep at it.
- **Exclamation point:** Your child may start to pick up cute little exclamations, such as "ta-da!" or "uh-oh!" So darn cute.

This is just a partial list of some of the more noticeable developments occurring. If your child is a little ahead or behind this list, please don't worry just yet. Your child's development is a marathon and not a sprint. The items on the list are generalities for babies of this age. The other main factor to remember is, like with their physical development, babies often do things in spurts. They may be behind the curve on a specific skill, and then suddenly they can do it without a problem.

Live boldly. Laugh Loudly. Love Truly.

Play as often as you can. Work as smart as you are able.

Share your heart as deeply as you can reach.

—Mary Anne Radmacher

Chapter 9

Crib Notes

- Your child will continue to change, and you must change with him as parents.
- As your infant nears his first birthday, he will be pulling up and trying to walk a little on his own. Make sure he practices in a safe place.
- Continue to keep a regular sleep schedule and sleep routine for your child to help him get a good night's sleep. Factors at this age that make babies restless sleepers include teething and possibly an overactive little mind as they learn new skills.
- Separation anxiety will peak in the 10–18 month range. Be honest and match your words with your actions. Say goodbye to your child, and then assure him you will be back. This issue can be hard on both of you!
- Manage your child's tantrums as best as you can. Keep him rested and properly fed, and keep him out of situations that you know from past experience will cause trouble.
- Your baby will love playtime and exploring the world around him. Be his playmate and his guide to shapes, colors, and words that will be fun for him.

CHAPTER 10

Mom and Dad

I may have mentioned this, but when you introduce a baby into your relationship, everything changes. Your relationship with your BRP is now a long-term thing. Whether you're married, divorced, or separated, you two now share parenting responsibilities and will most likely be together in some capacity at your child's activities—pre-k, kindergarten, 1st grade, 5th grade, 8th grade, high school, and college graduations—and probably at her wedding. It is quite daunting when you stop to think about it, and hopefully this is something you considered before the two of you decided to procreate. Incorporating your child's needs and best interests and placing them ahead of your own is now the *new* normal. Making sure you and your BRP are working together in unison is so important to your child. As we discussed in Part 1, there are many ways and situations that can create a happy, healthy child. But far and away the best situation for a child is to have two loving parents looking out for her every day. So, with that thought planted firmly in your mind, let's take a look at some relationship skills you may want to work on.

The Relationship

Relationship skills aren't like skills you might work on for an athletic or business pursuit. They are often less visible, and harder to acquire. They sometimes involve some of the toughest "skills" you can work on. Parenting only exacerbates the situation, because instead of caring for and building a relationship between two people, you now have three people to consider. It just makes it all the harder that one of them is a defenseless infant! Babies and kids in general thrive on a stable and predictable home environment. This has been proven time and again. They need someone they trust, someone they can count on to be there for them. You and your BRP are ideally those people.

The relationship skills we're discussing will hopefully be practiced by both you and your BRP in the spirit of cooperation toward a common goal: raising a happy, healthy child. What skills are they exactly? Well, they mainly revolve around the concept of sacrifice. Sacrificing your time, your resources, and your very self for the benefit of others. Because a total commitment to your family means sometimes (very often) putting those in your family before yourself. But you will also need to work on the tried and true "forgiving and forgetting." Because when we talk about relationship skills, it isn't about finding ways to have a perfect relationship where there are no fights or anger toward one another. This type of relationship doesn't exist as far as I know. No, these skills are more useful in navigating those ups and downs that come with having a long-term relationship with another imperfect person like yourself, "warts and all." This much is true: you need to love and accept each other for the unique individuals that both of you are. But don't use this as a shield to protect you from the pains of self-examination and improvement. You wouldn't mind if your BRP becomes a sweeter, more understanding person, and the same goes in the other direction. Knowing who you are, your areas of weakness (areas that can improve!), and working hard at improving those areas are great qualities for relationship building.

Let's start at the beginning. It seems like a logical place! We will take a minute to explore the most basic relationship skills. Because it is one thing if two people are in a relationship and split up and fight over who gets to take the painting the two of you bought on a whim. But if two parents permanently split apart and move, they disrupt their child's world in a big way. So though recent research suggests children with split parents can recover, it does throw children into a tough one or two year crisis period that isn't pleasant for anyone. So let's look at these relationship skills. These are the ones that you use if you want to keep a relationship going therefore we will not be exploring the finer points of name-calling, getting under someone's skin, and the art of *Gotcha!*" No, these fine skills do not apply here. Instead, we will discuss two of the most basic ones: listening and communication.

It's a Fact, Baby!

Is the number of American households that are married above or below 50 percent?

In a 2011 article, the NY Times disclosed that only 48 percent of U.S. households consist of married couples, down from 78 percent in 1950.

Listening

This one is easy, right? You just take out the ear buds and listen. Well, it seems like it may be more complex than all that. Truly listening can be even more complex when babies are around. Those little guys have no respect! They will cry when the mood strikes them, making it difficult to discuss the arc of your and your BRP's relationship. When in doubt, I like to make a list. So it's time for you to listen with your eyes and take in this list on listening:

- **Quiet, please:** When your significant other is talking, you need to focus. First, don't interrupt. Since it is likely you have not mastered the art of mind reading, she may be going to say something you didn't expect. Also, constantly cutting someone else off before she gets to complete her thought is a control thing, and can quickly raise the temperature of the conversation as the frustration builds. So while you are sitting quietly, process the actual words that are being spoken. Do not use the time to come up with your rebuttal argument. I know it's tempting, but resist.
- **Avoid traps:** Simply because you are sure you are right, don't sit and reflect on your greatness. Don't avoid or change the subject if it is an uncomfortable one, and call her out if she attempts the same. Lastly, the popular "I'm not discussing this" is no good for you two. It may prevent the pain of digging into a battle now, but I guarantee the issue at hand, not discussed, will bubble to the surface eventually. How long can you keep the lid on the boiling pot?
- **Moment of clarity:** While words are flowing into those things attached to the side of your head, make

sure you fully understand them. In an argument where strong emotions are in play, it's possible that you are not expressing yourself clearly. Before you jump in and attack, make sure you know the point your BRP is making.

- **What are we fightin' for?**: Ask yourself, "What are we really fighting about?" If you are in a figurative back-street brawl about dirty dishes left on the counter, then perhaps there are other issues concerning the two of you? What are they? If you can figure them out and address them, then you will be getting somewhere. Or, if you find yourself in a situation where you simply *have* to play in your Tuesday night basketball league, ask a simple favor. Then turn around and don't abuse the favor by going out drinking with the guys after the game while your BRP watches your bundle of joy. Your friends are not that funny, and your rapidly fading athletic skills are probably not paying the mortgage. So what are you guys fighting for? Make sure you do not allow small, selfish pleasures to become major issues in your relationship.

- **Lend me half an ear**: Remember in school when you tuned your teacher out to doodle or daydream? It is like you set your mind to snap to attention only if you heard your name. Well, some people (this is usually us, guys) tend to listen with a partial ear only to see if our lady is mad at us, upset about something, or is just sharing. Depending on which category our ear places the general tone of the conversation (am I in trouble?), we may tune out. But your BRP may be trying to tell you something important, so make an attempt to actually listen.

We are going to assume for optimism's sake that you love your BRP and have the ultimate goal of maintaining a positive, long-term relationship with her. So you don't want to have your head in the clouds when she is subtly communicating to you that she has been feeling depressed, or feels overwhelmed by life in general. So up your game in this important area and stay tuned in to what message is being delivered. This isn't just for your and your BRP's health. Study after study has shown that depressed parents are less nurturing to their children, which has been linked to poor health and developmental outcomes among those children. Parental depression has also been linked to concrete safety hazards like improper use of car seats, a lack of fire safety equipment, and a lack of electrical safety in the house. See, I will guilt you into being happy in no time.

Love seems the swiftest, but it is the slowest of all growths.

No man or woman really knows what perfect love is

until they have been married a quarter of a century.

—Mark Twain

Clear Communication

This part of a relationship is just as difficult as listening can be. I understand not wanting to get into the area of what I have heard referred to as "counselor-speak," where you say things like "I want to validate your feelings" or "How does this situation make you feel?" To some degree I think this makes you sound like a disinterested bystander in your relationship, instead of an emotionally invested participant. But there *is* something to carefully watching how you fight with your BRP. The when and how you approach a tricky conversation can truly be the difference in a productive fight/conversation versus a bunch of hurt feelings and name-calling that leaves you right where you started. When you fight dirty by not addressing the real issues at hand or not accepting blame and asking for forgiveness, the problems remain unresolved and often the fighting can escalate. Now how can your child grow up in a healthy environment when you two are throwing things at each other all the time? So watch yourself and your BRP for signs of fighting techniques that will usually escalate, rather than solve the problems occurring in your relationship.

- **Name (calling) game:** The basic thrust of this is that your true meaning or message can be totally obstructed by the words used. For example, if you choose to start your sentence with a reference to a female dog, and then say, "and you never let me hang out with my buddies!" the fact that the two of you are having a disagreement concerning your guy time and how much is appropriate has been tossed out the window. She may have stopped listening after the first portion of your sentence where you insulted her.
- **Admiral Ackbar:** Stars Wars enthusiasts will recognize the Admiral and his signature line, "It's a trap!" For those who could care less about Star Wars, just know that trapping your BRP into having an argument with you at the start of a long car trip, or as you sit down for a cross-country flight is considered playing unfair. Then she is faced with the choice of giving in or starting a fight with you about the topic, potentially ruining your vacation.

- **I don't care:** What I mean by this is don't say this to your BRP. If you find yourself saying this fairly often—or vice versa—it probably means that you have a certain amount of apathy toward each other in your relationship, which is not one of the ingredients for longevity.
- **Sarcasm:** I hate to have to cover this, but I promised to give you my best advice. I have a large sarcastic streak and enjoy irony, sarcasm, and the like. What this says about me I am not sure, but I am sure that throwing large amounts of sarcasm at your BRP is not an effective communication tool. The undertone to sarcasm tends to be that the sarcastic sender is of high intelligence, while the receiver is just not quite as sharp. It also tends to piss people off. There are enough emotions flying around without the added irritant of being sarcastic toward one another.
- **What's on your mind?:** So if you want to discuss something in particular with your BRP, be plain and honest about it. In honest language, state what is on your mind in as straightforward a manner as possible. "Honey, I think you are doing X too much, and I want to discuss it with you."
- **Try to say "I":** The experts often advise, when you are having tough conversations, to start with "I." Like "I feel you are attacking me" and "I would really like it if you wore lingerie more often."

If you can incorporate these tips, there is a decent chance that when the two of you fight, you may actually learn something from it instead of just seeing who can be the most creative in his or her insults. When you do fight, try to fight fair—or at least make some attempt to see your BRP's point of view, instead of focusing strictly on "winning." Try to put yourself in her position. Have empathy for her. Make an attempt to get out of simply defending your position, and try to see the issue from where she is sitting. Not to go all Zen on you here, but sometimes you have to lose to win (a.k.a. stay together) in the long run. As is often the case, the solution between the two of you will lie somewhere in the middle, and compromise will be required on both of your parts. Remember, now there is a child involved it's not just the two of you who will be affected by the long-term health of your relationship with your BRP.

Getting Back to Normal

Now that your baby's a few months old, you may find yourself asking, "When will things get back to normal?" Really? That is your question? Because I thought I was painting a pretty good picture that you have entered a brave new world, not a picture that you would be returning to your old, boring ways. It is time to sharpen your focus on the future, and redefine what your "normal" is. The quicker you accept and love your new reality, the easier it will be. You just signed up for a lifelong commitment to another person. You will use all of your tools, including emotional, physical, and financial, to attempt to ensure this child's success and happiness. You have no guarantee that you will be successful. But that's what makes us human and is so confusingly great about being a parent. For many, there is a time from conception going forward when they would gladly give everything they have for their child, and no matter the outcome, would not trade it for the world. So we all know that change is tough. People fall back into bad habits, start smoking again, regain weight they worked so hard to lose, but let's give it all to get this one right. It's not about being perfect; it is about knowing you did all you could. So embrace the changes as they come. Don't worry, if you don't love the current situation, it will change soon enough. Your new "regular" is not regular at all. It is a chaotic mess where you are balancing what needs to get done (too much) by balancing time and resources, including your own sanity. So for those of you looking to "get things back to normal," that is okay, as long as you totally redefine what that means.

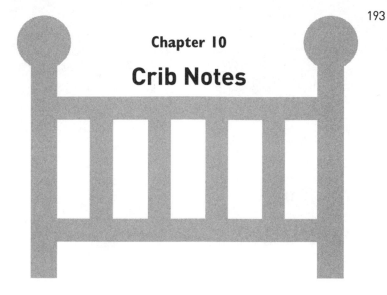

Chapter 10

Crib Notes

- Your relationship with your BRP is at a new level now that the two of you share a child together. Bringing a child into the world together and the responsibility that comes with it will change your relationship. You need to focus on your child's needs now. There are three people in the family who need love and attention, and your child needs it most of all!

- Because of this long-term relationship, you will need to approach your significant other with care and respect when difficult subjects need to be discussed.

- Listening is one of the most critical relationship skills you can develop. Try to really listen to each other, put yourself in her shoes, and understand what she is trying to get across to you.

- The flip side of listening is clear communication. Clearly express your thoughts and concerns when bridging tough topics.

- If all other avenues are not helping, you may want to consider consulting a relationship counselor.

- The answer to your disagreements will often lie in compromise.

CHAPTER 11

Parenthood

Here at "Dude" HQ in Georgia, we have several closely held beliefs. Most of them are complete nonsense, such as the Wesley Snipes *Passenger 57* classic inspired "Always bet on black." The roulette wheel has taught us this lesson many times. But there are a few that have held up over time. One of these few is that there are many different ways to raise a healthy child. Some parents seem to have it down cold, only to have their kids turn out all wrong. Other parents seem clueless, only to have their children become high achievers on their chosen path in life. Here we will look at some parenting styles for you to think upon. Think of it as a menu where you can take what you like and leave the rest. Hopefully, as your child's parent, you will have superior insight into his heart and soul. You will know his strengths and weaknesses, as there is a chance they might mirror some of your own through the magic of DNA. So keep that in mind as we take you on a tour of some of the best—and worst— parenting styles.

Different Parenting Styles

Parenting style used to seem so simple, if you feel like there is any kernel of real life reflected on TV. Kids responded pretty well to their parents, and if they did get into trouble, it was more of the "gee Dad, I'm real sorry, I didn't know we couldn't ride our bikes in the street" kind. In today's world it seems the indiscretions are much scarier, and kids are using technology to create different ways to misbehave faster than parents can figure out what is going on. But, as long as kids have been misbehaving, parents have been trying to figure out ways to prevent it.

The purpose here is not to push you to think about your parenting style. Many styles can be effective, though the research out there certainly seems to have come to a conclusion on which basic style is the best. Research has shown there to be four basic parenting styles that almost any creatively named trend or parenting book would fit into. If and when you discover parental differences of opinion, you need to discuss these differences among the adults and present a united front. Of course, this gets more important down the road! Here is an introduction:

1. **Neglect/Uninvolved:** Nothing to see here really. I promised to give you all four, and this is one of them. Basically the parents are neither demanding the child to grow or behave, nor are they responsive to the child's needs. There really is nothing of value to discuss here, except to say a quick prayer for the kids born into this situation.

2. **The Spoiler:** This is the parent that cannot say "no" to his kids. On the infrequent occasions that he

attempts to stand his ground, his young child will often respond, in scientific terms, as a "spoiled brat." As opposed to the neglectful parent, this parent is almost overly responsive to his child's wants and needs, but does not challenge his child on his standard of behavior and conduct.

3. **Yes, Sir!:** In this world, the parent will set very strict rules and boundaries that are not to be crossed. He imposes a high standard of strict rules, and punishment is usually handed down swiftly and forcefully, without discussion. But he may not be very aware or responsive to his child's emotional needs.

4. **The Authority:** This parenting style is described as the best of the choices by many. It, as you have probably guessed by now, combines the best of the styles. Parents who operate in this box both set boundaries and standards for their children, while still being responsive to their needs. Instead of harsh punishment, these kids are more likely to get a lecture on why their behavior or particular act was unacceptable. Severe punishment will only be handed down in extreme cases of misbehavior.

However, there is one more recent parenting style that is growing in popularity: the helicopter parent. A helicopter is a whole new kind of parent who either cannot or will not let his kids do anything by themselves. Imagine, if you will, a mother bird that, instead of eventually shoving her babies out of the nest, encourages them to stay there while she takes care of everything. These parents are almost *overly* responsive to their children's needs; in this way they will step in any time it appears their child might have any negative experience.

In addition, sometimes parents will need to have tough conversations with their kids, or you and your BRP may have to allow your child to fail at something. You may have seen it coming, or even warned your child. But if he refuses to listen, sometimes all you can do is let things run their course and be there for him on the other side. This is not a tool to be overused. It is more for a relationship of situation where you love someone so much, you have to help him forward through a difficult situation, even if it requires you to go against your natural instinct of helping and protecting those you love.

Now we have covered the basic four styles of parenting. Very few parents use purely one style. More likely it is a blend of two or more, depending on what comes naturally to you. How you parent may also depend on your child and what behavior he is exhibiting. Ultimately you would mainly parent in the emotionally responsive yet challenging zone, and if somehow you could manage to stay there, your consistent message would lead to a certain predictability and stableness that children usually respond well to. But you'll still need to change the rules and boundaries as your child grows up.

No matter what parenting style you choose, or how you and your BRP decide to raise your baby, it's important to keep one idea in mind: It has been said by a couple of different coaches in professional sports, "We treat everyone the same—fairly." I think this is a brilliant concept that applies directly to the parenting experience on many levels. Because in this quote it is implying that what is fair for each individual is not always the same. You alone as your child's parent gain a sense of what works for your unique child, as you know so many details of your child's life and where he is in his development. You know when a firm hand is required, when a hug will be just the thing, and if a little spoiling may be called for. Just remember that different situations constantly arise, and you need to be ready. If you choose a one-style-fits-all parenting style, that is fine. Just know *why* you are doing this and the alternatives that are out there. If you choose to fairly consider them and ultimately reject them, then you will be a better parent for it.

Treat a person as he is, and he will remain as he is.
Treat a person as if he were where he could be and should be,
and he will become what he could be and should be.
—Jimmy Johnson

The Answer to Raising Children

It is easy to agree that one of the most basic answers to successfully raising your child is to love them. Nobody would argue with that. Fortunately, children are a pretty lovable sort, so most parents are already a step ahead. But life is a tricky thing, and children seem to bring out these little idiosyncrasies in life. So now your job is to not only raise your child, but to continue to strive for self-improvement.

Parenting is more of an art form than an equation, and each person expresses himself differently. Like art, all of these different expressions can have their own unique greatness. But as children grow older, they come built-in with a contradiction meter, and they can very accurately sense when you are practicing what you preach, and when you are just preaching. It is understandable to want your children to not have some of the struggles that you may have had to overcome yourself. Tell your child to wear sunscreen on a sunny day, but do not apply any to yourself, and you can predict the first thing they will ask: "Why aren't you putting any on?" This principle will apply throughout life, including to the more complex questions later on. Go to a family cookout with your teen, drink a few beers, and then drive home. Chances are, he's going to notice. So the important lesson here is not only to love your child, but use the love you have as fuel to not only tell your child what to do over the years, but to also show him the path. This may require some painful adjustment on your part, but all of the lessons you want to instill in your children will fall flat if you have no credibility on the subject in their eyes.

At the same time, you have to be strong parents. As your children grow, part of the art of parenting is to attempt to develop some feel for when to let your children go it alone and when to step in. If you can be strong enough as parents to allow your children to learn to fend for themselves, then you have set the table for them to flourish. From my time parenting, I think the realization has hit me somewhat that endlessly heaping hollow advice on my kids is of limited value. They are not going to take such banal advice as "do your homework" as it comes down from on high. But if I can teach them how to analyze situations, think for themselves, and strive for the desired outcome, then this is something they will take with them anywhere life's journey may take them, whether their room is clean or not. So, I am not recommending that you force your infant to hunt and gather for his own food. But look for ways aid to in your child's development by allowing him to grow and tackle age appropriate tasks on his own.

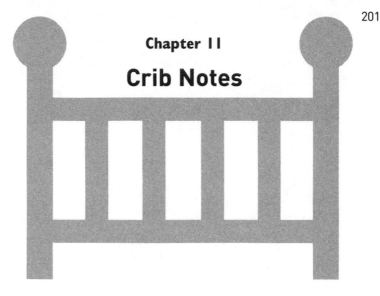

Chapter 11

Crib Notes

- One way to continue to develop as a parent is to read up on different parenting ideas that are out there in books, magazines, and on the web. You can take the ideas that fit with your parenting philosophy and incorporate them into your relationship with your child.
- There are four basic styles of parenting. These four vary in the way we respond to our child's emotional needs and how strictly we enforce rules and boundaries upon him.
- As a parent of a young child, you will have control of the relationship. As your child gets older, part of the responsibility will fall on him and how he reacts to the situations life presents to him and the help you provide to him.
- Set a solid example for your child to follow. Parenting is a tough job, and you will make mistakes. The important part is to keep giving your best to your child.

PART 4

One Year and Beyond

Like sand through the hourglass, time will continue to march forward. And as your child grows older and begins to do really cool things like sleep through the night, your life will be affected. If you have been gasping for some shuteye, then you will be pleased to know that she can accommodate this request, and even during the nighttime hours! In addition, your child will gain mobility and communication skills, and she will want you to fill the role of playmate.

CHAPTER 12

Year One: Milestones and Beyond the First 12 Months

During the first few weeks of your child's life, milestones may have included things like your baby successfully producing some poop for your nose's delight. As she got older, things like recognizing you and babble that faintly resembled "Mama" or "Dada" became important. Some of the bigger milestones, like the first time your child talks back to you, fails a test, or takes your car without permission, are far off in the future. So at this point we will give you a glimpse into the future at some of the more important upcoming events happening between ages one and two.

Physical Developments

So this one is probably quite predictable. Your child will grow. But do you know by how much? No? I knew you needed me for a reason. Over the first year, your beautiful baby should grow somewhere between three and five inches over this time frame. Your child, in a strange coincidence, will also gain three to five pounds during this time period. In other developments, toddlers will get stronger and become balanced walkers. Soon after, the jumping and running (away from you while in the local shopping mall) is soon to follow.

Talking

They say the quiet ones are always the troublemakers. Well, your child will understand ten times the number of words that she can actually speak by the time she is around fifteen months old. Soon, when she reaches age two, you will know about the troublemaker part. By the age of two, most babies are equipped with a vocabulary of about fifty words.

Social Developments

Your child is a little social being. While she isn't old enough for a Facebook page, she will still form a strong attachment to you, your BRP, and other family members. Your child will also bond with any regular caregivers that she sees on a regular basis. This is another reason that the teacher turnover rate is so important if you use a daycare facility. Constant change with the caregiver causes babies some stress.

Eating

Your child will continue to require a balanced, healthy diet with all of the nutrients her body needs. This will include proteins, carbohydrates, vitamins, minerals, and even some healthy fats needed for normal growth. A sound strategy for kids of this age is to not really worry about the exact amount they are eating at each meal, simply to make sure that there are plenty of healthy alternatives around. Children of this age have not developed bad eating habits, so they will usually just eat until they are full. As to the question of specifically what do they eat, you will find the usual suspects: fruits, vegetables, and dairy. Milk, eggs, and other sources of protein are important. Just make sure whatever she is eating has been prepared properly as to not be a choking hazard to your child. Hot dogs and grapes served "as is" (without being cut up into small pieces) are especially dangerous.

It's a Fact, Baby!

True or False: The American Academy of Pediatrics recommends whole milk for children between 1–2 years of age.

False. In 2008, the AAP starting recommending 2% milk for one- to two-year-olds. This is mainly due to the rise in the fat content of American diets, and the corresponding rise in overweight and obese American children.

Sleeping

Your child should still be sleeping somewhere between twelve to fourteen hours daily, with roughly 80 percent of those hours coming at night. This is a guideline doctors use; your child may vary. Somewhere along the spectrum of one to two years of age, your child will begin to nap less. If she was maintaining a schedule of two daily naps, this will eventually be consolidated into a single nap daily. This is all gearing you up for the biggest change of all: when your young one stops napping altogether. Then you will feel like you have taken a step backwards in your "me" time.

It's a Fact, Baby!

In tests, what percentage of toddlers could open a "childproof" bottle?

In tests, about one out of five toddlers could open a cap labeled as "childproof." Just goes to show why you always have to keep track of your infant.

Toddlers: Fun and Frenetic

When your child reaches age one, you can begin to consider her a "toddler" if you would like. If you are in my camp, you can quit the always annoying practice of giving your child's age in months, even though they are over the age of one (for the record, I am 472 months old as of this writing). Anyway, at this age your toddler, thankfully, will be frenetic *and* fun to care for. As she grows toward age two, she will begin to get her own ideas, have her own thoughts, and both want to be independent and dependent at the same time.

While your toddler will be exploring her new physical capabilities, such as running really fast (and occasionally falling) and throwing things (like your cell phone), she will also be testing the limits of her power over you. She may stand on top of the dining room table. She may run away from you and outside while completely naked. She will emphatically tell you "*no*" and throw quite impressive tantrums. And she will do all of these things to see exactly who is in charge in this house. So while she does not want to pay the bills, she is more than willing to boss you and your BRP around and have a chauffeur, maid, and on-call playmates. And just because it is called "the terrible twos" doesn't mean some children do not get a head start.

So what should you and your BRP do now? Bow down to the new little king or queen? I think not. Here are some tried and true parenting strategies for your little terror, um, toddler:

- **Previews are the best part:** Give your little girl a laminated copy of the schedule for the upcoming week. Or, since she probably cannot yet read, fill her in on what's coming up for the day. "First we are going to the store, then . . ." You get the idea. Feed her enough intel to let her little brain know what she will be doing today. Then she will let you know what she objects to, and the negotiations will begin!
- **Stick with it:** You are going to make rules, and that will be like waving a bright red cape in front of an angry bull. Your toddler will want to break the rule, in turn breaking your spirit and placing herself at the top of the food chain. I know she is really cute, but don't fall for it. If the rule you have created allows only one hour of cartoons per day, then stay with it. And when your toddler lies on the floor and has a total breakdown to the point where a stranger entering the home would suspect you of being a "big meanie," still stick to it. Otherwise, in a few short years, your

eight-year-old will be loose with a cell phone and
your credit card.

- **Ms. Independent:** Give your little princess some
(controlled) freedom. There are going to be things
she wants to do that will be messy or something that
she is just not quite ready for. Do a little preplanning
to let her do some of these activities in a manner that
is acceptable to you. Giving her some ways to learn
and express herself is a good thing, and you will have
some fun too.

- **Keep it real:** When I say this, I mean keep your
expectations and your planning for your day-to-day
realistic. If you know your child will self-destruct like
a Mission Impossible message after three hours at the
mall, don't expect her to be able to last any longer
than normal just because you have a lot of shopping
to do. She doesn't care. There may even be some shopping trips where you have to give the "abort" signal
shortly after arriving at the mall. This is back to redefining what control and planning is when you have
kids. All plans are subject to change!

- **Renew:** Don't forget what we discussed way back
in the book's introduction. If you have separated the
responsibilities where one parent is 100 percent work
and the other is 100 percent childcare, you are going
to look at each other every once in a while and think,
"They have it so easy compared to me." Well, neither
role is necessarily easier than the other, just different.
What you both need to do is quit worrying about
the other person and remember to regularly schedule your personal activity of renewal. Is this ringing
a bell? Meditate, paint, exercise, read, whatever it is

you have selected to keep you sane. Get back at it, so when your toddler tells you "NO!" for the 79th time today, you will be able to reach back, take a deep breath, and keep your cool.

Your child really is a sponge of sorts at this age. So instead of watching hours of *SpongeBob SquarePants*, try to work with her on some educational skills that will get her headed in the right direction for the future. There are several age-appropriate websites (*www.babytv.com* comes to mind!) that will help you out if you feel you have no idea where to start. You can work with your child on basic reading and sound skills, and don't be afraid to introduce her to writing as well, even if her earliest efforts are more scribble than prose. Her fine motor skills will allow her to hold a crayon and scribble, but trying to teach her shapes and letters will most likely result in frustration until she gets to be one-and-a-half years old or more. Research and personal experience has shown that you probably want to set a time limit on formal learning (10–15 minutes) but if your child seems willing to keep going, then by all means, nurture her inner Doogie Howser. More playful learning activities such as on the computer can be less structured.

You can see how the changes and development that take place change as your child gets a little bit older. Gone are the days of "baby's first . . . everything." Now every funny sound she says and her laugh are still just as charming, but she is also taking on more complicated tasks like walking and expanding her vocabulary beyond just a few basic words. These feisty little guys and girls will want to begin to assert themselves and take control of their environment, which is a good and positive thing, as long as they do not take control of you. You may have to stretch and grow as a parent also. For the last year, you have been in charge of taking care of every want and need of your baby, making sure she is happy and healthy. But now as your child discovers things like cupcakes and mommy's jewelry drawer, you are for the first time going to be telling your little angel "No"—and it's a word that you will be saying a lot.

It's a Fact, Baby!

True or False: It is normal for your child to bang her head repeatedly on the wall or other surface?

True. Believe it or not, up to 15–20 percent of babies and toddlers are head bangers. Bonus fact: boys are about three times more likely to do this. I guess that's not a total surprise. The banging can start at a young age, and they may not grow out of it until around the age of three.

Chapter 12

Crib Notes

- Your child is growing older, and will now be working on more complex developmental activities like walking, talking, and coloring. Of course she will continue to grow and develop physically as well.

- Your child will begin to develop socially. Just place some age-appropriate toys and another toddler in a playroom and watch. It will be fun for everyone!

- Your child's diet will begin to include more regular foods. Make sure you are offering her healthy foods to ensure she receives proper nutrition.

- When your child gets to this age, she begins to assert herself. Make sure to set rules and boundaries and be consistent with following them.

- Do *not* forget to take care of yourselves as parents. Find that special activity that re-energizes you and renews your strength and outlook on life and make time for it.

Afterword: Ready for More?

Depending on when exactly you picked up this book, you were a scared, tired, and substantially uninformed dad. Hopefully now that you have digested the contents of the book, you are only scared and tired! We have covered a lot of ground within these pages, and I hope you have found some value in the facts and figures coupled with the real world experiences I have shared with you. The fact that you are actively working to learn more about your role as a father is wonderful and moves you right to the head of the class. Remember that change is constant in the parenting world, and that the best thing you can do for your child is provide a stable environment for him and let him know with both your words and your actions that he can count on you. Not every minute of every day as a parent will seem magical to you; just know that it's the norm. The magic of parenting to me is thousands of special moments that occur over time that weave a special relationship between you and your child. So what are you waiting for? It's time to put down the book and go enjoy being with your family. Best of luck!

Appendix:
Additional Resources

Since I already admitted this in *Dude, You're Gonna Be a Dad!*, there is no shame in typing this again: I don't know everything. Okay, it still hurts to type that sentence. In addition, even if you read through this entire book about fatherhood, you may still need other resources to take advantage of, which brings us here—to the additional resources section. So in that vein, allow me to point out a few places where I found really good information for dads:

Christiandads.com: For those looking for a little divine inspiration, this is a good site. I mean, I hope someone is up there laughing at me, right?

Fathers.com: This is a good website that deals with things like how to handle today's entertainment media with your kids, how to communicate with your children, etc. It is more of a straightforward "dad" website, but I can't give you all fringe sites.

Greatdad.wordpress.com: Here is a site for the new dads. It handles things like tactics for handling separation anxiety, and how to navigate a "play date" with one of your child's friends. Remember when we just went over to our friend's house and came home "by dark"?

Onetoughjob.org: Finally, someone who isn't afraid to use a little humor in the title of their website. The job of being a dad is tough, and there is nothing wrong with saying it. Check out the sections on "Taking Care of Yourself," and if you are on the road for work, there is a section called "Tips for Travelling Dads" you should look at. Good stuff.

Zenhabits.net: Yes, there is the tiniest bit of hippie tendencies in me. Actually, it is some sort of hippie/Buddhist vibe that comes out every once in a while. I think most of us would profit from some silent focus at least once a week. But since I cannot even get into the Lotus position, I am linking to this site, which is chock full of good stuff for life in general, and for dads.

Index

About the Author

John Pfeiffer is a married father of three. He lives with his wife and kids in Atlanta, Georgia.